THE 84 GENIES OF POWER

Simple Secrets to Unleash the Miraculous Power of the Soul for Love, Money, and Power

Tristan Whitespire

Copyright © 2020 Tristan Whitespire

Disclaimer: The information provided in this book is not to be taken for medical or professional advice under any circumstances. By using the information contained in this book the user assumes full responsibility and agrees that Tristan Whitespire will not be held liable or responsible for any consequences that come as a result of the actions you take based on reading the information contained herein. The reader understands that no promises of success are made to the readers of this book. By reading this book you agree and understand that nothing said herein is meant to give medical, legal, or financial advice and should not be used in place of medical, legal or financial advice from a qualified expert. If you are in need of legal, financial, or medical help seek professional help and do not use the information in this book as a substitute for the guidance and advice of certified, qualified experts under any circumstances. Always be sure that you adhere to and obey the government, the laws, and the authorities of your country.

CONTENTS

Title Page	1
Copyright	2
Fulfill Your Will With The 84 Genies of Power	11
The Power of the Genies	14
The Story of Hercules and the Journey of the Soul	16
The Mystery of the 84 Genies	18
The Ritual Method	20
Summary of the Ritual Method	25
Genii of the First Hour Aries	27
Tarab (TAH-RAHB)	28
Sigil of Tarab	29
Misran (MEES-RAN)	30
Sigil of Misran	31
Labus (LAH-BUS)	32
Sigil of Labus	33
Kalab (KAH-LAHB)	34
Sigil of Kalab	35
Hahab (HAH-HAHB)	36
Sigil of Hahab	37
Marnes (MAHR-NES)	38
Sigil of Marnes	39

Sellen (SEH-LEN)	40
Sigil of Sellen	41
Genii of the Second Hour Taurus	42
Eglun (EGG-LOON)	43
Sigil of Eglun	44
Zuphlas (ZOOF-LAHS)	45
Sigil of Zuphlas	46
Phaldor (FAHL-DOOR)	47
Sigil of Phaldor	48
Rosabis (ROE-SAH-BEES)	49
Sigil of Rosabis	51
Adjuchas (AHD-JEW-KAHS)	52
Sigil of Adjuchas	54
Zophas (ZOH-FAHS)	55
Sigil of Zophas	57
Halacho (HAH-LAH-KOH)	58
Sigil of Halacho	60
Genii of the Third Hour Gemini	61
Sezarbil (SEH-ZAHR-BILL)	62
Sigil of Sezarbil	63
Azeuph (AH-ZOAF)	64
Sigil of Azeuph	65
Armilus (AHR-MILL-US)	66
Sigil of Armilus	67
Kataris (KAH-TAH-RIS)	68
Sigil of Kataris	69
Razanil (RAH-ZAH-NIL)	70
Sigil of Razanil	71

Bucaphi (BOO-KAH-FEE)	72
Sigil of Bucaphi	73
Mastho (MAHS-TOE)	74
Sigil of Mastho	75
Genii of the Fourth Hour Cancer	76
Eisnuch (ICE-NOOK)	77
Sigil of Eisnuch	78
Suclagus (SOOK-LAH-GUHS)	79
Sigil of Suclagus	80
Kirtabus (KEER-TAH-BUHS)	81
Sigil of Kirtabus	82
Sablil (SAHB-LIL)	83
Sigil of Sablil	84
Schachljl (SHAHKLE-JILL)	85
Sigil of Schachljl	86
Colopatiron (KOH-LOH-PAH-TEE-RON)	87
Sigil of Colopatiron	88
Zeffak (ZEH-FAHK)	89
Sigil of Zeffak	90
Genii of the Fifth Hour Leo	91
Nantur (NAHN-TUR)	92
Sigil of Nantur	93
Toglas (TOE-GLOSS)	94
Sigil of Toglas	95
Zalburis (ZAHL-BOO-REES)	96
Sigil of Zalburis	98
Alphun (ALL-FUN)	99
Sigil of Alphun	101

Tukiphat (TOO-KEY-FAHT)	102
Sigil of Tukiphat	103
Zizuph (ZEE-ZOOF)	104
Sigil of Zizuph	106
Cuniali (KOO-KNEE-ALL-EE)	107
Sigil of Cuniali	109
Genii of the Sixth Hour Virgo	110
Sialul (SEE-AH-LOOL)	111
Sigil of Sialul	113
Sabrus (SAH-BRUCE)	114
Sigil of Sabrus	115
Libabris (LEE-BAH-BREEZE)	116
Sigil of Libabris	117
Mizgitari (MEAZE-GIH-TAR-EE)	118
Sigil of Mizgitari	120
Causub (KAW-SUB)	121
Sigil of Causub	122
Salilus (SAH-LEE-LUHS)	123
Jazer (JAHZ-AIR)	125
Sigil of Jazer	126
Genii of the Seventh Hour Libra	127
Tabris (TAH-BREEZE)	128
Sigil of Tabris	129
Susabo (SUE-SAH-BOH)	130
Sigil of Susabo	131
Eirnilus (AIR-KNEE-LUHS)	132
Sigil of Eirnilus	133
Nitika (KNEE-TEA-KAH)	134

Sigil of Nitika	136
Haatan (HAH-TAHN)	137
Sigil of Hataan	139
Hatiphas (HAH-TEA-FAHS)	140
Sigil of Hatiphas	141
Zaren (ZAH-RIN)	142
Sigil of Zaren	143
Genii of the Eigth Hour Scorpio	144
Zeirna (ZAY-AIR-NAH)	145
Sigil of Zeirna	146
Tablibik (TAH-BLEE-BIK)	147
Sigil of Tablibik	149
Tacritau (TAH-KRIH-TAO)	150
Sigil of Tacritau	152
Suphlatus (SUE-FLAH-TUHS)	153
Sigil of Suphlatus	154
Sair (SAH-YEAR)	155
Sigil of Sair	157
Barcus (BAR-KUHS)	158
Sigil of Barcus	160
Camaysar (KAH-MAY-ZAR)	161
Sigil of Camaysar	162
Genii of the Ninth Hour Sagittarius	163
Phalgus (FALL-GUHS)	164
Sigil of Phalgus	165
Thagrinus (TAH-GRIN-US)	166
Sigil of Thagrinus	167
Eistibus (AYE-STEE-BUS)	168

Sigil of Eistibus	169
Pharzuph (FAR-ZUFF)	170
Sigil of Pharzuph	171
Sislau (SEAS-LAO)	172
Sigil of Sislau	173
Schiekron (SHAY-KRON)	174
Sigil of Sheikron	175
Aclahayr (AHK-LAH-HAH-YER)	176
Sigil of Aclahayr	177
Genii of the Tenth Hour Capricorn	178
Hahabi (HAH-HAH-BEE)	179
Sigil of Hahabi	180
Phlogabitus (FLOW-GAH-BEE-TUHS)	181
Sigil of Phlogabitus	183
Eirneus (AIR-KNEE-US)	184
Sigil of Eirneus	185
Mascarun (MAHS-KAH-RUN)	186
Sigil of Mascarun	187
Zarobi (ZAH-ROE-BEE)	188
Sigil of Zarobi	189
Butatar (BOO-TAH-TAR)	190
Sigil of Butatar	192
Cahor (KAH-HOAR)	193
Sigil of Cahor	194
Genii of the Eleventh Hour Aquarius	195
Sisera (SEAS-AIR-UH)	196
Sigil of Sisera	197
Torvatus (TOR-VAHT-US)	198

Sigil of Torvatus	200
Nitibus (KNEE-TEA-BUS)	201
Sigil of Nitibus	202
Hizarbin (HEE-ZAR-BEAN)	203
Sigil of Hizarbin	204
Sachluph (SAHK-LUHF)	205
Sigil of Sachluph	206
Baglis (BAHG-LISS)	207
Sigil of Baglis	208
Labezerin (LAH-BAY-ZER-EEN)	209
Sigil of Labezerin	210
Genii of the Twelfth Hour Pisces	211
Papus (PAHP-US)	212
Sigil of Papus	213
Sinbuck (seen-buck)	214
Sigil of Sinbuck	215
Kasphuia (KAHS-FOO-EE-AH)	216
Sigil of Kasphuia	217
Zahun (ZAH-HOON)	218
Sigil of Zahun	219
Heiglot (HEY-GLOT)	220
Sigil of Heiglot	222
Mizkun (MEASE-KOON)	223
Sigil of Mizkun	224
Haven (HEY-VEN)	225
Sigil of Haven	226
The Perfection of the Soul	227
Explore More Magick	229

FULFILL YOUR WILL WITH THE 84 GENIES OF POWER

The magick that you will discover in this book is fast, easy, and effective. This magick works by connecting you to tremendously powerful forces that are born from the depths of the human soul. When called, these intelligent forces come quickly, eager to fulfill all of our needs in life. The rituals you will find here are short, but powerful enough to transform your entire reality and restructure it into the life that you desire.

If you are used to feeling out of control in your life, as if no matter how hard you struggle you just can't seem to get ahead, these genies have the power to change that. When you summon them, you are summoning ancient, long forgotten powers that dwell within the human soul and inspire humanity to greatness. With the unique method you will find in this book, you will be given the gift to tap into that greatness and discover ancient secrets that have been locked away in the human soul for far too long.

Within these pages you will discover 84 uniquely powerful spirits that give you the power to discover love and romance, develop psychic abilities, protect the ones you love and hold dear, as well as to make others respect you.

When you call the simple, ancient words of power you will discover within this book, you will instantly awaken mighty angelic forces that hear your call and swiftly come to your aid to fulfill your will in all things which you ask of them. You may feel a shudder of tremendous power as you intone these words of power and the forces of heaven bend down to answer your calls. You will feel loved, cared for, and utterly safe when you perform this magick. There are no demons or evil spirits being invoked here. These are forces of ancient light and divine power whose purpose is to uplift the soul of humanity.

No one knows the true origin of this magick, its origins are perhaps more than a thousand years old and were written down for future generations by a great 19th century magician known as Eliphas Levi. Yet, although many great minds have poured over the text he translated, they still found the powers to be cryptic and difficult to understand. Without any type of rhyme or reason behind their ordering. It is here, within the pages of this book, that you will discover a clear and simple explanation of their powers that will enable you to put them immediately to use in your everyday life and, like the ancient alchemists, turn the metaphorical lead of your life into gold.

When you scan your eyes over the Hebrew letters and sigils you will find in this book, you are subconsciously tapping into tremendous powers of light that have worked magick for mankind for thousands of years. Regardless of whether you believe in angels or God it matters not. The power works automatically, just like turning a key in a car will start the engine. All there is for you to do is to follow the simple instructions and easy as baking a cake, you will witness your world change according to your will.

You may pause here if you like and flip through the pages of the book, looking at all of the powers that are presented here for you to choose from. Over 84 powers are at your fingertips. Regardless of what you desire to bring into your life you are likely to find power enough to spare within these rituals. Whether you desire to increase your physical energy, become more confident, increase your willpower to finish your projects, banish bad habits, attract potential romantic partners, or attract abundance and prosperity, you will find those powers here. You may wish to become an expert at divination, develop clairvoyance, or gain the ability to make wise plans that bring you success in whatever area of life you choose, if so then you will also find those powers here for you to choose from.

As you turn the pages of this book and read on, you will discover all that is possible for you. It is certainly not by accident that you picked up this book, that you are reading these words. Somewhere within these pages is a gift for you, a gift that has the power to transform your life in delightful ways that you may have only previously dreamed of. There are no lamps to rub and you certainly aren't limited to only 3 wishes. With the 84 Genies of Power, you are being given the key to success in life. So turn the key and open the door to authentic spiritual power.

THE POWER OF THE GENIES

When you hear the word "Genies" you may immediately get ideas of a person rubbing a lamp and a blue ghost-like being comes out and offers 3 wishes. Or you may get the image of Arabic spirits called Djinn. The spirits you will find here are neither of those. These powerful, intelligent, and loving spirits you find here can be described as being the personified embodiment of the virtuous qualities of the human soul. I hesitate to go into theory behind how and why this magick works because I know that few will be interested in it, but I believe some theory is necessary to fully appreciate this magick.

The genies you will discover here have their origin within the human soul in much the same way that angels have their origin in God. These genies are therefore always with us, residing within the depths of our soul as a spiritual potential, waiting for us to call them into being to help us with every aspect of our life. When you call upon these genies during the ritual, you may become aware of a powerful and loving presence that gently hears your desires and then diligently sets about to fulfil your will for you.

Why do they work on our behalf and what do they get from it? Surely there must be a balanced give and take in all magick? The beauty of the magick you find here is that these genies are born to serve the human soul. The service of the human soul is their reason for being. For they are literally born from the human soul the same way musical harmonies are born from a keyboard or the strings of a guitar. Normally, these genies remain as unnamed forces quietly working within our soul, and only arising when there is a need to perform a great work in our life that will give us progress towards fulfilling our destiny.

It is said that to know the name of a spirit or force is to gain control over it. This is exactly what we are doing with this magick. When you call the genies by this method you are harnessing forces of raw, creative power and energy within your soul and sending it forth to do your will. These genies will never refuse your requests to them, it is their sacred duty to fulfill your will. Regardless of how big or small your requests seem, these powerful forces will move into action immediately and set about arranging the circumstances of your life in a harmonious and non-disruptive way to bring about the fulfillment of your will.

My favorite part of this magick is that as we perform the magick and achieve the fulfillment of our desires we are also gaining spiritual growth. Performing this magick is like effortless weightlifting for your soul. With each request you make your soul grows stronger and you will begin to develop the powers of the genie that you call on so that you can access that power more easily in the future. Their powers will grow progressively stronger within you until one day you may no longer need to call upon the genie at all to fulfill that particular power as you will have integrated with that aspect of your soul represented by the genie. When this happens you will become capable of wielding that power for yourself by intention alone.

THE STORY OF HERCULES AND THE JOURNEY OF THE SOUL

My style of writing is to keep the intro to my books very short and to the point so that you can get right into the magick. I have found that this is much appreciated by my readers. No one buys a magick book to learn boring and obscure history lessons, but rather to gain access to authentic power that can change your life for the better. And that is what you will find in this book. But before we get to the heart of this book it helps to know a little bit more about the magick.

These genies are said to have originated from an ancient Greek book called the Nuctemeron which was translated into English by a great French occultist named Eliphas Levi in the 19th Century. In his translation, very cryptically we are shown 12 groups of spirits with 7 spirits in each group. We are told that they somehow relate to the 12 allegorical labors of Hercules and represent the "works of initiation" whatever that means. For many years occultists have studied these spirits and tried to derive meaning and practical uses for their powers with varying results. Through a series of fortunate synchronicities their meaning became clear to me in a unique way that I have not seen revealed anywhere else. Those revelations given to me through research and deep meditation form the basis of the magick you will discover within this book.

My understanding of the true powers of these spirits came from researching the story of the 12 labors of Hercules (traditionally known as Herakles – which means "Glory of Hera"). Hercules or "Herakles" can also be translated as "Glory of the Soul", for I discovered that Hera represents the soul. In the traditional myth Hera, who is known as the Queen of the Gods, decided to make trouble for Hercules (the human soul) by causing him to become temporarily insane. In his insanity he commits the crime of killing his wife and children. As punishment for his crime he is kicked out of heaven and is sentenced to spend 12 years on Earth and while there, to be subject to the will of Eurystheus who signifies the ruler of the material world. The ruler of the material world tells the Hercules (who represents the human soul) that he has to complete 12 tests or labors which means traveling through the 12 signs of the zodiac. This represents the journey of the soul's evolution as it travels through the signs of the zodiac. He is told that if he succeeds, he will become an immortal which means a highly evolved, perfected soul. This story has strong similarities to the story of Adam and Eve being kicked from the Garden of Eden.

So, the story goes that he endures 12 tasks or labors that are meant to destroy him. As he passes through each of these 12 labors he learns new lessons, gains new power, and evolves towards become a perfect immortal. This symbolizes the journey of the soul as it passes through each of the 12 signs of the zodiac. As the soul journeys, it learns the lessons of each sign and gains all the skills and abilities that each sign affords to it and thus the soul evolves towards ultimate perfection and reunion with the Source of this Universe.

THE MYSTERY OF THE 84 GENIES

Now enough with the history lesson. Where do the 84 Genies factor into all of this? Seven is the number of completion and perfection. There are 7 days of the week, 7 major planets, and 7 major chakras within the human body. These all correspond with the 7 genies in each of the 12 signs of the zodiac.

All 7 aspects of our soul (which are represented by the 7 chakras) must pass through each of the 12 zodiac signs. As these 7 aspects of our soul pass through the signs they each learn their own unique lesson and develop their own unique gifts and powers that the cosmic energies present within that zodiac sign gives to them. When all 7 aspects of our soul travel through all 12 signs of the zodiac and learns all of the lessons, we become a perfected soul, an immortal master of light.

These 7 genies each represent the powers and lessons of the soul in each sign of the zodiac. The beauty of this is that even without passing through the 12 signs and having to struggle to master each of them we are still able to tap into and access all 84 powers of the perfected soul through genies. And by working with these genies we naturally can learn the lessons each of them has to offer and thus evolve towards perfection even as we fulfill our will and our desires on Earth.

Through this magick we gain access to the powers of wealth, love, knowledge, discernment, power, and so many other gifts and powers of the soul. We are, like Hercules, both human and divine in nature. We are at once both human flesh and eternal soul. As mentioned previously, Hercules means "Glory of the Soul" and that glory spoken of is the light and power that these genies embody. This is why they are called "personified virtues".

These genies are the light, radiance, virtue, and glory of the soul in embodiment. They are sparkling crystals of light of inestimable value. This book is your invitation to touch, experiment, play, learn, and most importantly, grow as you interact with these ancient and sacred forces of power. Know that as you perform this magick, you are fulfilling the purpose of every soul in this human life. This purpose is growth and evolution. And ultimately, it is this growth and evolution of the soul that is the true goal and purpose of all magick.

THE RITUAL METHOD

In the pages that follow you will discover the 84 genies arranged in groups of 7 and categorized according to the astrological sign that they represent. Through hours of researching the powers and comparing them to the degrees of the zodiac and their meanings, I arrived at the realization of their proper order. You will find that their powers perfectly corresponded with the astrological position that they represent.

These 84 sigils are empowered to work for us through the use of various names of God and angels written in Hebrew. Don't let this scare you. You do not need to be able to read Hebrew to use this magick. Hebrew is a special language of great spiritual power and simply by scanning your eyes over the Hebrew letters during the ritual, you will be connecting on a soul level to ancient, powerful, divine forces of light that have the power to fulfill your will. The names of the 84 genies have also been converted into Hebrew writing to add to their potency and accessibility. Beneath the name of the genie in Hebrew, you will also find the name of each genie written in a special angelic script called Malachim which adds additional potency to the magick. You do not need to be able to read or understand any of the words on the sigil. As long as you scan your eyes over the sigil, it will work.

You will also see on the sigils some strange looking lines and shapes within bottom triangle and the two stars on the right and the left. These are the sigil of the genies drawn three times. This sigil aids you in connecting to the genie that you are calling on and only needs to be scanned by your eyes in order for it to work. This is visual magick. By seeing the sigil and calling the names using the simple ritual described here, you will quickly and easily be empowered to put the magick into motion.

Do not feel worried about pronouncing the Hebrew words or the names incorrectly. You cannot get this wrong. As long as you scan the sigil using the method that I will explain below, the forces and energies of the sigil are automatically with you and aware of you. At that time, even if you mispronounce their names, they will still sense your intent and will fulfill your will based on what your clear intent is.

After you find the genie that has the power that will help to bring you what you need, proceed to step one of the ritual outline.

Step one:

Tune into your feelings in the present moment. Contemplate the discomfort that inspired you to perform this ritual. You have a need. Feel the frustration of not having this need already fulfilled. Allow yourself to truly open up to your honest feelings in the present moment. This only takes a minute or less.

Step two:

Beginning at the very tip of where the upper triangle is pointing to (the top middle of the circle), begin to scan your eyes counter-clockwise (from right to left) around the words in the outer circle. You don't need to scan exceptionally slowly, but nor should you do this too quickly. Just gradually scan your eyes across the letters as you take in their shapes at a leisurely pace and know that you are in this moment connecting to powerful divine forces who have the power to fulfill your will.

Step three:

Look at the upper triangle. Within the triangle you see four rows of Hebrew letters. This is the highest name of God and is pronounced EE-AH-OH-EH. As you gaze into the triangle, letting your eyes rest upon the letters there, begin to chant EE-AH-OH-EH until you feel relaxed and peaceful. This connects you to the Source of all spiritual power in the universe.

Step four:

Briefly look at the name of the genie in the middle bar at the center of the circle. Then look at the shape within the bottom triangle briefly as well, this is the genie's sigil. As you do so, know that this is the spiritual force that will come forth and fulfill your request. Feel gratitude towards the genie for the help that you will receive from them.

Step five:

Here you will call the names that are written in the outer circle. Remember that you cannot get this wrong. You are already connected to these spirits because you scanned their names visually. The names are written phonetically to make for easy pronunciation. When you call the names you may do so out loud, vibrating the names with power, or you may call them quietly or silently inside your head. The most important thing is that you call them as if you are literally calling a friend or a person across the room to pay attention to you. Know that they hear you and are present with you the moment that you speak their name.

Say the words:

AH-DOH-NAI

EE-AH-OH

YICH-EH-AK-EV-CAH-HA

YITZ-OH-HAH-YAHV-TAH-HAH

YEE-YAH-HAH-GAV-LEE-HAH

GAH-DEE-YELL

TOO-VEE-YELL

OO-REE-YELL

RAH-FAH-EL

MEE-KAH-EL

GAH-BREE-YELL
YUH-DID-YAH
RAH-ZEE-YELL
YEH-OH-EL
NOO-REE-YELL
YAH-BAHM
EE-AH
OH-MEM
VEH-HOO

The words above stay the same in each ritual. The only thing that changes in each ritual is the spirit's name. So after saying the words of power above, we make our short call to the genie as shown below. This example uses the spirit Sialul:

Sialul!

Hear me Sialul!

It is my will that you _____. (state your will 3 times in 2 sentences or less)

Thank you Sialul! Go in peace.

You will see that you are instructed to state your will 3 times in 2 sentences or less. So lets say your desire is to get a new car. You would say, "It is my will that you bring to me a new car." And you will repeat that sentence 3 times before saying "Thank you Sialul! Go in peace!"

Step six:

Gaze at the sigil with a feeling of gratitude that your desired result has already come to be fulfilled. This step is absolutely essential to the success of the ritual. The more powerfully you feel gratitude for the results of the ritual (even though you cannot see them in physical reality yet) the more powerfully the ritual can manifest. See your results in your mind as already being real. See yourself enjoying the results and let gratitude well up from within your heart like light and pour this light into the image as you perform the next step. This step usually only takes about a minute or two but you can extend it longer if it feels good.

Step seven:

While still feeling that feeling of gratitude, chant YAHA-DONAHI (YAH-HAH-DOH-NAH-HEE) 3 times while gazing at the sigil to close the ritual.

This name connects you to divine abundance and good luck.

SUMMARY OF THE RITUAL METHOD

1. Sense your feelings in the present moment regarding your desire.

2. Scan the outer circle of Hebrew letters.

3. Look at the upper triangle and chant EE-AH-OH-EH until you are relaxed.

4. Scan the genie's name in the middle and briefly scan the sigil in the lower triangle.

5. Say the words:

AH-DOH-NAI

EE-AH-OH

YICH-EH-AK-EV-CAH-HA

YITZ-OH-HAH-YAHV-TAH-HAH

YEE-YAH-HAH-GAV-LEE-HAH

GAH-DEE-YELL

TOO-VEE-YELL

OO-REE-YELL

RAH-FAH-EL

MEE-KAH-EL

GAH-BREE-YELL

YUH-DID-YAH

RAH-ZEE-YELL

YEH-OH-EL

NOO-REE-YELL
YAH-BAHM
EE-AH
OH-MEM
VEH-HOO

The words above stay the same in each ritual. The only thing that changes in each ritual is the spirit's name. So after saying the words of power above, we make our short call to the genie as shown below. This example uses the spirit Sialul:

Sialul! Hear me Sialul! It is my will that you _____. (state your will 3 times in 2 sentences or less) Thank you Sialul! Go in peace.

6. Gaze at the sigil with a feeling of gratitude that your desired result has already come to be fulfilled.

7. Chant YAHADONAHI (YAH-HAH-DOH-NAH-HEE) 3 times while gazing at the sigil with gratitude to close the ritual.

GENII OF THE FIRST HOUR ARIES

TARAB (TAH-RAHB)

Role: Genius of Extortion

Planet: Moon in Aries

Sephirah: Yesod

Day: Monday

Greek God: Selene

Chakra: Sacral Chakra (Second Chakra)

Powers: Tarab is a genie that gives us the power to stake our claim on what we need. To go after and obtain the things we need with focused drive, dedicated force, and energy. If you find that you have a tendency to be lazy, Tarab can help you to overcome that and secure the things that you desire to have in life with gusto.

If you are doubtful of your ability to gain what you desire in life, Tarab gives you the confidence and motivation you need to help you acquire the things that you desire in life whether it is a relationship, money, a new job, or any other physical things. You will still have to get up and work for what you want but with the energy and power of Tarab flowing through your life you will find that it is vastly easier to succeed. Gone will be the feelings of heaviness, sluggishness, and sloth as well as doubt and indecision. You will become sharp, precise, and energetic. A powerful force to be reckoned with, overcoming all obstacles that stand in the way of obtaining what you desire. This is the energy of a conqueror staking his claim on a land and making it his kingdom.

SIGIL OF TARAB

MISRAN (MEES-RAN)

Role: Genius of Persecution

Planet: Mars in Aries

Sephirah: Geburah

Day: Tuesday

Greek God: Aries

Chakra: Root Chakra (First Chakra)

Powers: Misran is a warrior's spirit. Blazing the trail towards whatever he desires to do. Even if the whole force of the world were to block his path and tell him he cannot fulfill what he desires, Misran would overcome them. This is a tremendously powerful energy that gives you the power to take quick, decisive, and motivated action towards fulfilling your desires in life. If you find that you overthink things and hesitate in your life Misran is the power that overcomes that. This is the energy of focused speed and directed force towards a specific goal.

When you call on Misran you will gain the power to overcome obstacles that stand in the way of your dreams quickly and effectively. You will no long worry about what other people may think of your decisions or hold back due to a feigned sense of politeness. You will come, see, and conquer. Misran gives you the power to fulfill your personal will despite all opposition and setbacks.

SIGIL OF MISRAN

LABUS (LAH-BUS)

Role: Genius of Inquisition

Planet: Mercury in Aries

Sephirah: Hod

Day: Wednesday

Greek God: Hermes

Chakra: Third Eye Chakra (Sixth Chakra)

Powers: Labus gives us the power of strong communication and decisiveness. When we call on Labus we gain the power to make quick, accurate, and effective decisions. This is the power to dismiss and overcome all nonsense and useless information that stands in the way of learning what we desire to learn. We gain the power to be confident and forthright in speech and communicating with others. Labus gives us the power to speak our mind with confidence. To communicate and live our truth without shame and without backing down.

If you need mental inspiration and new ideas you can call upon Labus and you will find that helpful and useful ideas come to your mind that help you with your current or new projects. Labus gives us great initiatory and visionary powers to conceive of new and revolutionary plans or inventions and carry them out with drive and passion.

SIGIL OF LABUS

KALAB (KAH-LAHB)

Role: Genius of Sacred Vessels

Planet: Jupiter in Aries

Sephirah: Chesed

Day: Thursday

Greek God: Zeus

Chakra: Throat Chakra (Fifth Chakra)

Powers: Kalab gives us the power to discover our inner gifts and talents and the drive and willpower to develop them further. With the power of Kalab our gifts and talents can bring us great success. We gain the drive and motivation to expand onto the world stage and showcase our skills and talents for all to see. Kalab also helps us to discover what work we do best and what work will make full use of our talents and bring us happiness and fulfillment.

If we are feeling lazy and neglect developing our talents and gifts further, Kalab has the power to give us the discipline to commit to self-development. If we are searching for a job or an opening that allows us to showcase our skills and talents to the world then Kalab can help us discover the perfect fit for us, helping us to land the job that makes the most of all of the inner gifts that we have to bring to the world and achieve success thereby. Kalab also restores our optimism and positive thinking regarding the future.

SIGIL OF KALAB

HAHAB (HAH-HAHB)

Role: Genius of Royal Tables

Planet: Venus in Aries

Sephirah: Netzach

Day: Friday

Greek God: Aphrodite

Chakra: Solar Plexus Chakra (Third Chakra)

Powers: Hahab is a Genie of pleasure. She inspires us to be confident and bold in seeking out and discovering what brings us pleasure. Physical pleasure and sensuality is a part of earthly life. To neglect this part of our life is to forfeit the important lessons that having physical pleasure offers us. Hahab has the power to help us attract opportunities to experience sensual pleasure of all sorts whether that is delicious food, attracting a new lover, hearing beautiful music, or traveling to exotic and new locations. Hahab is all about experiencing the richness and variety of physical life on Earth and helps us to seek, find, and enjoy all opportunities for experiences which will bring us sensual delight.

SIGIL OF HAHAB

MARNES (MAHR-NES)

Role: Genius of the Discernment of Spirits

Planet: Saturn in Aries

Sephirah: Binah

Day: Saturday

Greek God: Kronos

Chakra: Crown Chakra (Seventh Chakra)

Powers: When we call on Marnes we gain the power of wisdom and decisiveness. This gives us the power to make wise decisions and to be confident in the decisions that we make. If you find that you second guess yourself often and have a fear of asserting yourself or following through with your dreams and desires, Marnes gives the power to overcome that fear.

Marnes helps us to discern the most profitable course to take when we are at a crossroads in life or need to make important decisions. He gives us the power of enhanced intuition when it comes to making choices in life. This is a very important power as each choice we make, even small ones that seem insignificant, can lead to a vastly different future. Set your intention, make it clear to Marnes what your goals are in life and he will help guide you to make the decisions that will manifest the life of your dreams and the fulfillment of your desires with confidence.

SIGIL OF MARNES

SELLEN (SEH-LEN)

Role: Genius of the Favor of the Great

Planet: Sun in Aries

Sephirah: Tipareth

Day: Sunday

Greek God: Helios

Chakra: Heart Chakra

Powers: Sellen gives us the power of charismatic leadership and the ability to rally others to our cause. He brings great confidence, self-assurance, energy, and boldness. Sellen has the power to make you shine with the bold, proudness of the sun and thereby attract others to your light. Sellen has the power to overcome fear, social anxiety, and indecision. He can help you transform yourself from being a follower to being a charismatic leader whom people look up to for direction and guidance.

If you are giving a speech or presentation of any kind or even entering a debate with someone, Sellen can cause you to radiate a compelling light of confidence and self-assurance from within which draws people to your light. If you desire someone to obey your wishes and do what you'd like them to do, calling on Sellen with method can make people compliant to your wishes and willing to please you whether they are higher or lower in rank or social status than you. This is a powerful ability to have so be sure to use it conscientiously and be careful to not abuse this power.

SIGIL OF SELLEN

GENII OF THE SECOND HOUR TAURUS

EGLUN (EGG-LOON)

Role: Genius of the Lightning

Planet: Moon in Taurus

Sephirah: Yesod

Day: Monday

Greek God: Selene

Chakra: Sacral Chakra (Second Chakra)

Powers: Eglun is a genius of adaptability and change. Too often we tend to get stuck and set in our ways and stubbornly refuse any type of change even when it is positive change. This hinders our personal growth and success in life. Most people prefer to stay in a familiar situation, job, or relationship that is uncomfortable but familiar than to move into a new, better, but unfamiliar one. We are creatures of comfort and this holds us back in so many ways and on so many levels.

Eglun, the Genius of Lightning give us the power, courage, and inner strength to break out of our comfort zone. She gives us the willpower we need to move on to bigger and better things in our life instead of staying stuck in the same dull routine. Here you gain the power to break free from oppressive or uncomfortable situations. The energy of Eglun is like the energy of The Tower card in the Tarot but in a more controlled way. Here, you control and direct this powerful energy of change in the way that you desire.

Eglun can also help you break free from writers block or any other creative blockages. Also to conquer the fear of showing your work and your true self, skill, and talents to the world.

SIGIL OF EGLUN

ZUPHLAS (ZOOF-LAHS)

Role: Genius of Forests

Planet: Mars in Taurus

Sephirah: Geburah

Day: Tuesday

Greek God: Aries

Chakra: Root Chakra (First Chakra)

Powers: Zuphlas gives us the power of endurance and continuing to move forward in life or in our projects we are working on despite all obstacles, all odds, and all setbacks. With the power of Zulphas, we simply keep moving forward at a steady, deliberate pace until we have accomplished what we have set out to do.

Here is the power of great patience. We may often avoid taking up a project because of how far away the goal seems or how difficult and tedious it appears to be. Though we will often find that once we begin that the task wasn't nearly as difficult, scary, or tedious as we first believed. Zulphas gives us the power to get over that first hump, that mental stubbornness and laziness that keeps us from starting a task. Then once we start he gives us the energy and staying power to endure until the end and the project or process is completed.

SIGIL OF ZUPHLAS

PHALDOR (FAHL-DOOR)

Role: Genius of Oracles

Planet: Mercury in Taurus

Sephirah: Hod

Day: Wednesday

Greek God: Hermes

Chakra: Third Eye (Sixth Chakra)

Powers: Phaldor gives us the power to see the large picture, to take a birds-eye view of a situation so that we will be able to successfully plot our course. This includes the ability to make clear and detailed plans and formulas or an outline that ensures success. Think of a sports coach or a warlord plots decisively his team's positions in the field. Or a chess grandmaster who can see the 10 or more moves ahead, and so can anticipate each and every obstacle that may arise.

On a more mystical level, Phaldor greatly increases our intuition and perception so that we gain insight into the future. This usually comes as a strong feeling or hunch about what the right move is to take next or what the next right step might be. In this sense, Phaldor can greatly enhance your divinations whether it be Tarot reading, scrying, dream work, or any other methods of obtaining mystical insight into the future.

SIGIL OF PHALDOR

ROSABIS (ROE-SAH-BEES)

Role: Genius of Metals

Planet: Jupiter in Taurus

Sephirah: Chesed

Day: Thursday

Greek God: Zeus

Chakra: Throat Chakra (Fifth Chakra)

Powers: Rosabis is a master financier. Think of a wealthy banker. Rosabis is shrewd, calculating, and know the true value of all things. Thinking of starting a project or business and want to know if it will be profitable? Rosabis can give you insight into what may work and what may fail. He gives us wisdom in all forms of investing whether it be an investment of our time, money, or emotions. As such, he can help us to "strike gold" in our projects and relationships and to gain true value and great rewards from our endeavors.

The value of this power cannot be overstated. Many people waste a great portion of their lives invested in sterile, fruitless activities that do little to no good for their lives, on the contrary, may even be harming them and their lives. With Rosabis you have the power to turn any such situation around in your own life by gaining the wisdom to know what actions are of value and which are not. This power can also be directed to others in our lives to get them to find value in their lives if they are invested in harmful or fruitless endeavors so that they see the error of their ways and gradually move in the direction of success.

Another application of this power is the power to increase our self-worth. If we have low self-esteem it is only because we have yet to see our own true value and the value that we can bring to others. Everyone is worthy, valuable, and has a unique gift or talent they were born to bring into this world. Call on Rosabis to discover your own value and sense of self-worth. This power alone can create a revolution in your life and lead to great positivity, good fortune, and success.

SIGIL OF ROSABIS

ADJUCHAS (AHD-JEW-KAHS)

Role: Genius of Rocks

Planet: Venus in Taurus

Sephirah: Netzach

Day: Friday

Greek God: Aphrodite

Chakra: Solar Plexus Chakra (Third Chakra)

Powers: Adjuchas is a genius of physical beauty. That is, the kind of beauty that can be seen, touched, tasted, experienced. From physical beauty gained through working out, to the artistic beauty of words on a page in a work of fine literature, and everything in between. Adjuchas rules the manifestation of beauty in all of its physical forms. From the subtle, erotic beauty of a lover's passionate touch, to the delightful beauty of a fine, exquisite wine. Adjuchas rules all manifestations of beauty's incarnation on Earth.

You can call on her power in any endeavor that needs the cultivation of beauty, or sensual delight such as in our sexual relationships, crafting any form of art, even the art of socializing. You can also attract more sensual beauty into your life by calling on her powers when you feel that your life is sterile, cold, square, and lacking of the vibrant delight of this Venusian energy.

You also have the power here to increase the beauty of your physical form and cause others to see you as beautiful and attractive. As well as seeing you as someone who can bring them sensual pleasure. This Adjuchas can therefore help you to attract new lovers to your charm. This works better for general attraction than for specific attraction but it is capable of working for both.

SIGIL OF ADJUCHAS

ZOPHAS (ZOH-FAHS)

Role: Genius of Pentacles

Planet: Saturn in Taurus

Sephirah: Binah

Day: Saturday

Greek God: Kronos

Chakra: Crown Chakra (Seventh Chakra)

Powers: The world can seem like a scary place for the soul. We are caught in the prisons of flesh. We are forced to work and labor for our food, clothing, and shelter and we have seen time and time again disaster striking here or there in the world, or maybe even in our own life and wiping away all of the possessions that have been gained through hard work. This creates a fear of loss as well and creates the idea that we need to hold on tightly to everything we have whether money or relationships in fear that we might lose them.

Zophas brings the power of faith in abundance. Physical things can be gained and lost. Sunny weather changes to rain, the stock market rises and falls, relationships come and go, but behind all of that is a continual source of endless abundance. It is the source of all good things. The true source of prosperity and wealth. Zophas gives us the power to connect with this source so that we have a deep conviction and understanding that we will always be taken care of. We will always be provided for in our life. Like deeply rooted trees that pass unharmed through all the changes of the seasons and are endlessly nourished by the elements.

This gives us the courage to try new experiences, travel to new and exciting places, try out new careers and ventures, give and share our earnings and possessions freely, and always having faith that no matter where we find ourselves in life we are connected to a source of good that will always protect us, care for us, and bring us good fortune in whatever situations or circumstances we find ourselves in. If you are going through a difficult time right now, you can ease your mind and free yourself from your fears by calling on Zophas to restore your faith in the goodness and abundance of the universe. When you do, you may find good things naturally begin to flow into your life. The lesson here is: everything always works out in the end.

SIGIL OF ZOPHAS

HALACHO (HAH-LAH-KOH)

Role: Genius of Sympathies

Planet: Sun in Taurus

Sephirah: Tipareth

Day: Sunday

Greek God: Helios

Chakra: Heart Chakra (Fourth Chakra)

Powers: Life is about relationships. The quality of our relationships with others and with the world around us determines the quality of our life to a large degree. Halacho is all about creating harmonious, stable, dependable, and lasting relationships. This includes everything from a relationship with our boss and work colleagues, to a relationship with our finances, or a relationship with a spouse or lover, and even our relationship with our physical body.

Halacho has the power to bring harmony, comfort, sympathy, understanding, and love to our relationships so that we have support, stability, and security in every aspect of our life. This gives us the power to settle disputes and disagreements in the work place, to strengthen a bond or relationship and enhance communication with our spouse or lover, to learn to live within our means and balance our finances so that we can build abundance, and to develop a balanced relationship with our physical body so that we feel comfortable in our skin. We will be led to the best types of workouts to do and the best types of foods to eat to get the type of body that we love and feel good about.

Halacho's power is to help us to feel completely balanced and harmonious in our connection to every aspect of our life. Our relationships are like a car, when it is tuned and harmonious, we are able to get to the place in life we desire to be smoothly and easily. Your environment and all within it should be supportive of you. Through the powers of Halacho you can ensure that it is.

SIGIL OF HALACHO

GENII OF THE THIRD HOUR GEMINI

SEZARBIL (SEH-ZAHR-BILL)

Role: Devil or Hostile Genius

Planet: Moon in Gemini

Sephirah: Yesod

Day: Monday

Greek God: Selene

Chakra: Sacral Chakra (Second Chakra)

Powers: Sezarbil, contrary to the name, is the Genius of social harmony. She is a great socialite, a social lubricant who is skillful at breaking the ice in awkward situations or resolving conflicts and easing hostility and arguments wherever they may flare up. If you are going to be in a situation where you need to reach an agreement with others or you need to resolve a conflict, call on Sezarbil to encourage resolution. The other person will likely become much more open and affable, and willing to come to a harmonious agreement with you.

This power has many out of the box applications that could really ease your life and save you money. You can use it for out of court settlements, marriage or relationship disputes, and more. Anywhere there is a conflict in communication or self-expression and you need to come to an agreement, use the powers of Sezarbil to reach a satisfying conclusion for all involved.

SIGIL OF SEZARBIL

AZEUPH (AH-ZOAF)

Role: Destroyer of Children

Planet: Mars in Gemini

Sephirah: Geburah

Day: Tuesday

Greek God: Aries

Chakra: Root Chakra (First Chakra)

Powers: Despite the scary sounding name, this genius is in reality very helpful. Azeuph is the genius of projects and creativity. Do you have trouble focusing on projects? Whether you struggle to get started on a single project or you find that you try to work on too many projects at once and end up accomplishing nothing, Azeuph can help you to find your perfect balance. Call on this powerful genius to learn how to stay focused and committed to a project until it is completed. Or if you do have multiple projects that you have to juggle, Azeuph will give you the energy and balance required to find balance as you spread yourself thin between them. This is the force of accomplishment and achievement. Conquering your projects like a boss and finishing them to perfection. I

The powers of this genius can also apply to any form of self-development that you seek to devote yourself to such as weight loss and so on. Anytime you lack the willpower and drive to start a project, task, or endeavor and see it through to successful completion, call on Azeuph to help you see it done.

SIGIL OF AZEUPH

ARMILUS (AHR-MILL-US)

Role: Genius of Cupidity

Planet: Mercury in Gemini

Sephirah: Hod

Day: Wednesday

Greek God: Hermes

Chakra: Third Eye (Sixth Chakra)

Powers: Armilus is a genius of knowledge. Need to learn a lot of information very quickly? Learning a new language or trying to perfect a new art form or hobby? This genius gives you the power to quickly learn and absorb vast amounts of information. This power of course has many applications and far reaching potential. The acquisition of knowledge is what allows us to grow and advance in all areas of life. With the powers of Armilus you can gain absorb and retain the knowledge you need to succeed at a test, gain a promotion, write a book, learn an instrument or any new skills at all.

With the powers of Armilus you can also become great at communicating your knowledge with others, with teaching and sharing knowledge in a skillful and entertaining way that people will understand and love. Knowledge is power. Whether you are sharing knowledge or getting knowledge and information, Armilus can greatly enhance your efforts and bring success.

SIGIL OF ARMILUS

KATARIS (KAH-TAH-RIS)

Role: Genius of Dogs or of the Profane

Planet: Jupiter in Gemini

Sephirah: Chesed

Day: Thursday

Greek God: Zeus

Chakra: Throat Chakra (Fifth Chakra)

Powers: Kataris has the power to cause others to respect you and warm up to you. If you have been mistreated, looked down upon, or disrespected by a person or group of people, calling upon Kataris can change their attitudes towards you to one of respect and even friendliness. In this way, Kataris can solve most social problems that we encounter.

Arguments, disputes, and wars of all kinds are usually caused by one person or a group of people insisting their way is the right way and the best way. The cause of this kind of thought is essentially due to misunderstanding of others and a lack of respect for others. Kataris has the power to open even the most stubborn and hard-headed people to you and your ideals. Even if they don't accept or agree with them, you can come to a mutually peaceful resolution.

Kataris also gives you the power to understand things from the viewpoint of another person. This allows you to, in a way, think how they think and feel how they feel. To understand their mind. This allows you to know how to gain friendship with and sympathy from others who otherwise might not have warmed up to you or helped you at all. From respect comes understanding. From understanding comes peace. From peace comes harmony which may even develop into love.

SIGIL OF KATARIS

RAZANIL (RAH-ZAH-NIL)

Role: Genius of the Onyx

Planet: Venus in Gemini

Sephirah: Netzach

Day: Friday

Greek God: Aphrodite

Chakra: Solar Plexus Chara (Third Chakra)

Powers: Greek legend has it that one day the Goddess of Love and Beauty, Venus was sleeping and Cupid (also known as Eros) cut her fingernails which then were transformed into Onyx. Razanil represents Onyx in the sense that he is a genius of love. She helps in all matters concerning love and relationships. Her specialty is helping you to attract a new and exciting, stimulating relationship into your life or with spicing up old relationships that seem to have lost their energy and passion.

Razanil can also transform you into someone who is seen as desirable to others. This is the power of seduction. This power works better when used for general attraction rather than for a specific person but you are welcome to invoke Razanil to focus her powers on a specific person that you desire and see how things develop as well. This is not mind control or interfering with a person's free will. It opens others up to seeing your beauty and charm, and makes you appear stimulating, exciting, and attractive to the other person. The only problem with this power is that you may find that you attract multiple lovers at once and must then choose between them. Although to some, that may not seem like much of a problem at all!

SIGIL OF RAZANIL

BUCAPHI (BOO-KAH-FEE)

Role: Genius of Stryges

Planet: Saturn in Gemini

Sephirah: Binah

Day: Saturday

Greek God: Kronos

Chakra: Crown Chakra (Seventh Chakra)

Powers: Bucaphi has the power to overcome fears and anxieties. If you find that you anticipate the worst in your life or that you are filled with vague or specific fears or anxieties, you can call on Bucaphi to banish them. He comes forth like a powerful spiritual wind to blow away negative and fearful thoughts and in their place leaves clarity of thought so that we can see things in our life as they truly are.

Bucaphi gives us the power to face life head on. To directly confront the things that we fear and overcome them. If you find that fear or timidity is holding you back in any area of your life call on Bucaphi to break through that barrier so that you can achieve success. It is said that the only thing we have to fear is fear itself. Bucaphi has the power to banish fear and impart confidence.

If you are feeling confused about any situation and that confusion is preventing you from making progress Bucaphi can also clear away the confusion surrounding anything in your life, bringing clarity to your mind to allow you to make progress.

SIGIL OF BUCAPHI

MASTHO (MAHS-TOE)

Role: Genius of Delusive Appearances

Planet: Sun in Gemini

Sephirah: Tipareth

Day: Sunday

Greek God: Helios

Chakra: Heart Chakra (Fourth Chakra)

Powers: Have you ever met a person who, like a chameleon, seems to blend in with whoever they are with at the time? Regardless of who they are socializing with they have an uncanny skill of fitting in and being liked. Mastho gives you the power to do this. If you will be in a social situation or setting in which you need to be liked or appear to be someone or something that you aren't Mastho can aid you in this. People will, for a time, believe that you are the person that you are projecting yourself to be. To put this to use simply call on Mastho and ask him to make you appear a certain way or ask him to make you blend in. Be sure to name the person or group whom you will be meeting and precisely tell Mastho how you wish to appear and what effect you want to have on the people you are meeting.

On the flip side of this power, you can also call upon Mastho to see through the delusive appearances of others. If someone is acting like someone that they really aren't, or you need to test the true character of someone in your life then Mastho will enlighten you to the truth of who that person really is. You can also use this power to perceive the true nature of any organization or group of people as well. This gives you the power of penetrating insight.

SIGIL OF MASTHO

GENII OF THE FOURTH HOUR CANCER

EISNUCH (ICE-NOOK)

Role: Genius of Agriculture

Planet: Moon in Cancer

Sephirah: Yesod

Day: Monday

Greek God: Selene

Chakra: Sacral Chakra (Second Chakra)

Powers: Eisnuch has the power of nurturing and making things grow. She is called the Genius of Agriculture and could perhaps quite literally be called upon to ensure the nourishment and protection of plants and/or crops. More practically for most of us though (unless you are a farmer) she has the power to nurture and nourish our relationships in life. It has been said that life is relationships, and when you think about it you find this to be true. Your parents, friends, spouse, job, everything is based on relationships. Often success or failure in life is determined on our connection to the right people.

If you would like to strengthen and nurture any relationship in your life to make it healthy and long-lasting then call upon Eisnuch. She will strengthen the two-way bond in any relationship. If you feel neglected or underappreciated, she can correct this and cause the other person to see you as valuable and cherish you more. She can also give you insight into the relationships in your life to teach you how you can strengthen them as well.

SIGIL OF EISNUCH

SUCLAGUS (SOOK-LAH-GUHS)

Role: Genius of Fire

Planet: Mars in Cancer

Sephirah: Geburah

Day: Tuesday

Greek God: Aries

Chakra: Root Chakra (First Chakra)

Powers: Suclagus is like a circle of protective fire surrounding us. If you ever get into a confrontation with someone or someone is threatening you, call upon Suclagus and often you will be able to diffuse the situation before it escalates any further, restoring peace. Although sometimes regardless of what you try, the situation does escalate. In such cases Suclagus can protect you from violence directed towards you from others whether of a spiritual nature (such as a curse) or of a physical nature by helping you to avoid situations in which violence may occur. Suclagus also can also fill you with metaphorical fire to make you brave, strong, and able to fearlessly face your enemies. You will be filled with a spiritual power and a righteous anger that will help you to conquer opposition, defend those you love, and restore peace and balance to situations of conflict all without resorting to violence.

This power may seem a bit vague because it can manifest in multiple ways as every situation of conflict is different, but you will often see the situation rapidly diffuse and harmony be restored.

SIGIL OF SUCLAGUS

KIRTABUS (KEER-TAH-BUHS)

Role: Genius of Languages

Planet: Mercury in Cancer

Sephirah: Hod

Day: Wednesday

Greek God: Hermes

Chakra: Third Eye Chakra (Sixth Chakra)

Powers: Kirtabus is a genius that helps with communication and understanding. If you feel that you aren't being understood or listened to and your message just isn't getting through, call on Kirtabus to inspire others to be more understanding of you. If you also feel that you aren't understanding someone else, why they are acting the way they are towards you or what their true needs are, Kirtabus can enlighten you.

Kirtabus, as his name suggests, can also help you with learning a new language. You may find that you can absorb the language intuitively and your understanding and fluency grows rapidly.

He also gives the gift of letters and can make you an eloquent writer or poet, with the ability to channel your thoughts and feelings very effectively and in a way that will get your message and feelings through to others clearly.

SIGIL OF KIRTABUS

SABLIL (SAHB-LIL)

Role: Genius who Discovers Thieves

Planet: Jupiter in Cancer

Sephirah: Chesed

Day: Thursday

Greek God: Zeus

Chakra: Throat Chakra

Powers: Sablil has the power to create financial security in your life. If you find that money tends to slip through your fingers or that you have metaphorical holes in your pockets, Sablil can give you the wisdom you need to increase your wealth and attract financial good fortune into your life. He has the power to enhance your intuition around matters of finance, investments, and career choices, helping you to find what is most profitable. If you are currently employed, he can strengthen your job security as well as helping you to get a raise or promotion.

Sablil can encourage others to be generous with you and lend freely. This includes causing employers to see you as a good investment and a reliable person who is of value to the company.

He can also of course, protect your property and things from thievery and reveal those who stole from you. He can also expose cheaters in relationships. He has the power to reveal the truth in various situations.

SIGIL OF SABLIL

SCHACHLJL (SHAHKLE-JILL)

Role: Genius of the Sun's Rays

Planet: Venus in Cancer

Sephirah: Netzach

Day: Friday

Greek God: Aphrodite

Chakra: Solar Plexus Chakra (Third Chakra)

Powers: Everyone deserves to be cared for and nurtured in a relationship. Yes all too often good people get caught in bad or unbalanced relationships where their partner doesn't seem to show much love or care for them at all. If you are caught in such a relationship you can call on Schachljl to either end the relationship and attract a more caring and loving one, or to transform your current partners feelings to be more loving with you.

This may take time so don't expect an instant miracle of affection. Although that could very well manifest when calling upon this powerful genius of love through this method. You can also call upon her powers to discover how you may express more love to another person or love them in a way that makes them feel secure and cherished with you.

SIGIL OF SCHACHLJL

COLOPATIRON (KOH-LOH-PAH-TEE-RON)

Role: Genius Who Sets Prisons Open

Planet: Saturn in Cancer

Sephirah: Binah

Day: Saturday

Greek God: Kronos

Chakra: Crown Chakra (Seventh Chakra)

Powers: Colopatiron is a genius of intimacy and self-expression in relationships. When we have been hurt in the past, we tend to close up and refuse to let anyone else in. Perhaps you are in a relationship that is lacking intimacy. You may be closed up to your partner and not know why. Or you may find that your partner refuses to open up to you. Colopatiron has the power to open our self-inflicted mental and emotional prisons to allow us to be open and vulnerable to others. To open up can be a scary thing but the growth of a relationship is (whether in business or romance) is impossible unless we open up and express our true needs and we understand the needs of our partner. Call on Colopatiron to increase intimacy and openness in your relationships.

Colopatiron gives us the confidence to open our hearts and minds and express our thoughts and feelings regardless of what people might say. By expressing ourselves honestly and truthfully, we can gain true fulfillment from life and create loving, successful relationships.

SIGIL OF COLOPATIRON

ZEFFAK (ZEH-FAHK)

Role: Genius of Irrevocable Choice

Planet: Sun in Cancer

Sephirah: Tipareth

Day: Sunday

Greek God: Helios

Chakra: Heart Chakra

Powers: Zeffak gives us the power of persistence. If you find that you make plans to accomplish things but struggle to carry through on them due to self-doubt or anything else, call on Zeffak to give you the power to stick strongly to your decisions. Zeffak represents the power to carry on in any endeavor despite setbacks or road blocks that we might encounter along the way. In this sense, he is a bit like the Hindu God Ganesha in the sense that he helps us break through and overcome obstacles on our path.

When you call on Zeffak you may feel a strong determination and resolution to complete whatever tasks or projects you call him to help you with. He also has the power of intuition and can assist us with finding the best solution to whatsoever problems that we encounter in life as well. This can be invaluable guidance and can save us hours, months, or perhaps years that might otherwise have been wasted searching for the way around a roadblock.

SIGIL OF ZEFFAK

GENII OF THE FIFTH HOUR LEO

NANTUR (NAHN-TUR)

Role: Genius of Writing

Planet: Moon in Leo

Sephirah: Yesod

Day: Monday

Greek God: Selene

Chakra: Sacral Chakra (Second Chakra)

Powers: The powers of this genius applies to writers of all types but most specifically to fiction writers. If you are struggling with ideas in your writing and are stuck with writers block call upon Nantur. She can send the fires of creative genius through your mind to break through creative blockages and stimulate ideas. If you feel afraid of self-expression and afraid that your creations may not be accepted by others, Nantur can break through that indecision. It is like children drawing. They don't worry about what others will think of their work and are not self-conscious at all. They draw for the pure pleasure of being creative and expressing their ideas. They are even excited to show their drawings to the world and hang them on the walls or the refrigerator. Nantur gives you that bold, expressive, unabashed spirit of creative joy and self-expression. The desire to create and for your creations to be seen and celebrated by all. And with the power of this genius, that is a very real possibility.

SIGIL OF NANTUR

TOGLAS (TOE-GLOSS)

Role: Genius of Treasures

Planet: Mars in Leo

Sephirah: Geburah

Day: Teusday

Greek God: Aries

Chakra: Root Chara (First Chakra)

Powers: In a highly competitive world, success is only given to those with the ambition, focus, passion, and drive to accomplish their desires. Everyone wants great things out of life but only the rare few have the power to charge forth, conquer, and claim what they desire with swiftness and confidence. We make excuses, we get lazy, we procrastinate, we believe its too difficult and give up early.

If these descriptions sound like things that you struggle with, Toglas can help you. Toglas is a powerful genie who gives us the ability to obtain whatever we desire in life through ambition, focus, and fearless willpower. If you are struggling to accomplish any goal and feel you are lacking that extra push or extra drive to accomplish what you desire in life, call on **Toglas** to spur you on, inspire you, give you that push. Toglas can turn you into a confident warrior who never backs down when pursuing your dreams and believes there is no obstacle too great to climb and conquer, you may even relish the challenge when his energy comes into play within you. The treasures of this world always go to those with the confidence and ambition to claim them.

SIGIL OF TOGLAS

ZALBURIS (ZAHL-BOO-REES)

Role: Genius of Therapeutics

Planet: Mercury in Leo

Sephirah: Hod

Day: Wednesday

Greek God: Hermes

Chakra: Third Eye Chakra (Sixth Chakra)

Powers: Zalburis is a genie that promotes balance. He has the power to remove all forms of stagnancy and blockages in our lives to restore a healthy flow of energy. If you are feeling stuck or blocked in any part of your life it is due to an imbalance happening on some level. Calling on Zalburis allows you to discover the origin and cause of that block and to remove it so that harmony and balance can be restored.

In Feng Shui and Chinese Medicine it is known that the cause of all our problems whether of body, mind, or life circumstances is due to an imbalance or blockage in the flow of life force energy (also known as Ki, Prana, or Chi). This theory states that when life force energy is flowing smoothly in our lives there is health of body, mind, finances, relationships and every aspect of our life. Zalburis is a master of restoring balance where there is imbalance and restoring the flow of energy where there is blockages.

If any part of your life is not working or you feel frustrated from achieving what you desire, call on Zalburis to remove these blockages and restore harmony and flow to your life. Sometimes this power work by clearing the blockage with no further work on your part but other times it works by simply showing you where the blockage is in your life and allowing you to manually work through and clear it to learn a life lesson.

SIGIL OF ZALBURIS

ALPHUN (ALL-FUN)

Role: Genius of Doves

Planet: Jupiter in Leo

Sephirah: Chesed

Day: Thursday

Greek God: Zeus

Chakra: Throat Chakra (Fifth Chakra)

Powers: Alphun is a genie who has the power to bring good fortune. In Greek mythology the dove is a symbol of Fortuna, the goddess of fortune and good luck. In images, the Goddess Fortuna is often seen holding a cornucopia that is filled with infinite golden coins or an infinite abundance of fruit. This is called the Horn of Plenty and is a symbol of infinite abundance.

Legend has it that the Horn of Plenty was created by the Zeus when he broke the horn off of his wet nurse who was a goatwoman named Amalthea. The horn was then blessed with the divine power to produce from within it whatever it's possessor desired. This is the reason that Alphun is called the Genius of Doves.

Alphun represents the inexhaustible energy of abundance. This is an energy that gives endlessly and generously without asking for anything in return. If you desire to achieve success, good fortune, and abundance in any area of your life call upon Alphun and then ensure you are open, receptive, and ready to receive the outpouring of abundance that so he so readily and generously pours out upon you in your life.

This power also lends itself to empowering you to express yourself clearly and with confidence in any situation and to be well received. Thing presentations, first dates, job interviews, or anywhere else that making a good first impression is essential. The other person with be filled with an innate liking for you and a sense of generosity welling up within them towards you. With this power you can bless all of your relationships with positivity, generosity, and good will.

SIGIL OF ALPHUN

TUKIPHAT (TOO-KEY-FAHT)

Role: Genius of the Schamir

Planet: Venus in Leo

Sephirah: Netzach

Day: Friday

Greek God: Aphrodite

Chakra: Solar Plexus Chakra (Third Chakra)

Powers: The power of Tukiphat is to open up the hearts and minds of others towards you. If you find that you are being neglected or treated coldly in any relationship whether romantic, business, or friendship, call on Tukiphat. She has the power to increase love and affection in an existing relationship or even to inspire strangers to treat you will kindness and generosity wherever you go.

If a romantic relationship has been damaged for any reason, often the heart closes off and the relationship dies. Tukiphat has the power to restore love, passion, and affection in a relationship that has gone cold. You may find that a new energy enters the relationship and refreshes it. And the old excitement of the relationship that you used to feel is reborn. No one deserves to be mistreated, ignored, or treated coldly for any reason. Tukiphat has the power to melt the coldest heart and open the hardest of hearts.

Another application of her power is to encourage others to give you a change. Whether you are applying for a job, trying to get a book published, or even asking someone out on a first date. Tukiphat has the power to open the hearts of others and warm them up to you so that they will be inspired to give you a chance.

SIGIL OF TUKIPHAT

ZIZUPH (ZEE-ZOOF)

Role: Genius of Mysteries

Planet: Saturn in Leo

Sephirah: Binah

Day: Saturday

Greek God: Kronos

Chakra: Crown Chakra (Seventh Chakra)

Powers: It has been said by many ancient sages time and time again, "know thyself". Yet it is much easier said than done. Who are we? What do we desire in life? And how can we go about getting it? Many people go through their whole life without knowing the answers to these questions. Then on the other hand there are those who do know who they are and what they most want in life but are too afraid to pursue it due to shyness and insecurity or a fear of standing out and being seen and noticed by others.

Zizuph is the genius who can help us to dig deep within our self and uncover our true desires as well as our true gifts and talents. He can help us to discover our self and to know our self and be secure in who we are. Once we have developed that solid foundation within, he can help us to express ourselves confidently and with self-assurance. To take away our fear of being seen by others and expressing our truth and pursuing our dreams with confidence and authority.

Zizuph can also help if we desire for our self or a creation of ours to get seen. If you find that you tend to go unnoticed or get passed over for things call on Zizuph to make you stand out from the crowd. If you are trying to promote a product or creation you have made Zizuph has the power to make it seen by others. It doesn't guarantee that they will like it, but it will get noticed.

SIGIL OF ZIZUPH

CUNIALI (KOO-KNEE-ALL-EE)

Role: Genius of Association

Planet: Sun in Leo

Sephirah: Tipareth

Day: Sunday

Greek God: Helios

Chakra: Heart Chakra (Fourth Chakra)

Powers: Cuniali gives us the power to find the perfect balance in interpersonal relationship. That balance consists in finding the happy medium between two polarities. The first polarity is being confident, assertive, bold, and dominant. The second polarity is being meek, humble, and allowing of others, of working as a team. When these two polarities are balanced then all relationships become effective. It is a balance between Yin and Yang that brings harmony.

If you find that you are having trouble being confident, speaking up, and standing up for yourself Cuniali can give you the confidence and inner power that you need to be bolder. If on the other hand you are being told that you are too overbearing, too forthright, or too aggressive, then Cuniali can help you find the perfect balance. It is hard to know what polarity you fall into on your own so it is easier to simply ask this genie to for balance in any relationships where things aren't working in your life, to perfect your connection with others in your life so that your relationships are effective in every area of your life and everyone can get what they want and need in a harmonious way.

This is a power whose value is far reaching. It is the power to master human relationships. When we have mastered the art of human relationships, we can succeed in any area of life that we choose. For what else is life if not relationships with others?

SIGIL OF CUNIALI

GENII OF THE SIXTH HOUR VIRGO

SIALUL (SEE-AH-LOOL)

Role: Genius of Prosperity

Planet: Moon in Virgo

Sephirah: Yesod

Day: Monday

Greek God: Selene

Chakra: Sacral Chakra (Second Chakra)

Powers: When we think of prosperity, we usually think of large flowing amounts of money or fancy card and lots of houses. While this can be an image of prosperity to some, to others prosperity could be just having two loaves of bread to eat instead of one. Or having one well clean and well running car than 5 fancy cars they don't even drive.

When we manage what little we have, even that little can seem like a lot. Give a glutton a piece of bread to eat and he might throw it on the ground and tell you to bring him a steak instead. Yet give a starting person a piece of bread and they might view you as if you were a god and feel immensely grateful. The power of Sialul is about managing what ever we have well and being satisfied and grateful for whatever possessions we have instead of forever seeking to gain more. Sialul gives us the power of quiet and simple contentment with our current lot in life and the ability to manage it so well that it feels that we are truly prosperous. Prosperity has many definitions, but when we are able to manage what we have in such a way that all of our needs are met, that is true prosperity.

It has been said by many that when we are faithful over a little, we will be given a lot. This also holds true here. Sialul gives us the power to manage well whatever we have and as we do so, we will find a steady, natural increase flowing into our lives. Gratitude creates abundance. And satisfaction can make a mansion out of a mud hut.

SIGIL OF SIALUL

SABRUS (SAH-BRUCE)

Role: Sustaining Genius

Planet: Mars in Virgo

Sephirah: Geburah

Day: Teusday

Greek God: Aries

Chakra: Root Chakra

Powers: If you find that you often give up too easily as your tasks or your to-do list, Sabrus has the power to help you to get it done. This is the power to have drive, determination, and willpower to conquer and complete all that you set out to do. If you find that your disorganized way of doing things is the cause, Sabrus can help you to sort yourself out and get all the details organized so that you can smoothly streamline your tasks and fulfill them with ease. This is the power to be steady, focused, disciplined, and methodical and never giving up until your tasks are done and your mission is complete.

SIGIL OF SABRUS

LIBABRIS (LEE-BAH-BREEZE)

Role: Genius of Hidden Gold

Planet: Mercury in Virgo

Sephirah: Hod

Day: Wednesday

Greek God: Hermes

Chakra: Third Eye (Sixth Chakra)

Powers: Libabris has the power to help you find hidden things of value. This power works on many levels and in many situations. If you are searching within yourself for hidden skills and talents or for self-worth and confidence, Libabris can help. It also helps when you are searching for what career or life path will be most fulfilling or financially profitable for you. This genie can lead you to discover that path. If you are trying to find a rare book or item, that is another rather obscure power that can be found here. And finally, if you are literally searching for hidden gold and treasure, you can call on this spirit to guide your steps. This works for actual treasure hunters, archaeologists, or even those searching for ancient texts and secrets from lost civilizations or societies. Libabris is a very useful genius and gives us the power to find anything that is lost or hidden that is of value to us or to the world at large.

SIGIL OF LIBABRIS

MIZGITARI (MEAZE-GIH-TAR-EE)

Role: Genius of Eagles

Planet: Jupiter in Virgo

Sephirah: Chesed

Day: Thursday

Greek God: Zeus

Chakra: Throat Chakra

Powers: Although eagles fly high across the expansive sky and can see from horizon to horizon from their high vantage point, they have a sharpness and precision of sight that allows them to see even the smallest mouse running across the ground before swooping down speed and accuracy to grasp it. Jupiter rules expansion and Virgo's influence is methodical precision. Mizgitari is a genie who gives us the power to balance both of these extremes.

This power is useful because it allows us to stay organized in our life and our projects by keeping the whole of the project in mind, even while working on the smallest of details. To see how the smallest detail fits into the larger scope of things and how the larger scope of things is composed of each precise detail. If you feel lost and directionless in your life, call on Mizgitari to help you remember the big picture and give direction in your life. This can unfold in a number of ways from reading something that guides you, or receiving guidance and insight from another person in your life or even a direct intuitive knowing.

If you are feeling overwhelmed at the thought of completing a task that seems to tiresome or big or too much to handle, call on this genie to help you to see the best place to begin working on the project. This power is also helpful when deciding how to accomplish a magickal goal. This genie can help you understand how to best accomplish any large goal by breaking into smaller steps and then working magick on each of those individual steps with in an orderly, methodical fashion until your larger goal is complete. Working in this way, there is very little we cannot achieve. Everything in life has a formula for success. Mizgitari can reveal to you that formula. As the great philosopher Seneca once said, "Luck is what happens when preparation meets opportunity."

SIGIL OF MIZGITARI

CAUSUB (KAW-SUB)

Role: Serpent-Charming Genius

Planet: Venus in Virgo

Sephirah: Netzach

Day: Friday

Greek God: Aphrodite

Chakra: Solar Plexus Chakra (Third Chakra)

Powers: Causub is strong with the powers of harmony. She can bring any arguments or bickering and disagreements to a harmonious resolution. Not only does she bring harmony to those who are at odds with each other she will also unite them and cause them to feel kinship, camaraderie, and sympathy for each other. If you find you are being mistreated, Causub can change the hearts of those who mistreat you and cause them to do a 180 degree change and seek to please and accommodate you instead. With this power you can warm the hearts of anyone you desire to you.

And finally, with her power to influence the heart of another, she has the power to encourage the blossoming of romance between you and another. This power works by opening the heart of another person to seeing what is attractive within you. It is similar to the effect of cupid's arrow which sparks love in the heart of the one you desire when they lay eyes on you, for they see you in a new light and they see beauty in you which they didn't perceive before.

SIGIL OF CAUSUB

SALILUS (SAH-LEE-LUHS)

Role: Genius Who Sets Doors Open

Planet: Saturn in Virgo

Sephirah: Binah

Day: Saturday

Greek God: Kronos

Chakra: Crown Chakra (Seventh Chakra)

Powers: Ever see those people who are super successful and yet when you look at their work it is full of errors or the quality is sub-par and yet, somehow, someway they are popular and successful? You may tell yourself that you can do what they do and easily. But for some strange reason, you don't. There may be a large number of reasons that hold you back but one of them almost certainly is overthinking the situations, trying to be a perfectionist, and therefore holding yourself back from achievement.

Often times we are our own worst critic, our own biggest obstacle. Our thoughts tell us that we aren't good enough, that we will never succeed, that we don't have the time or the knowledge or a million other self-sabotaging things. Salilus is a genius sets open the doors to our dreams by helping us to overcome this self-limiting nature. He gives us the power to simply dive in and work on our tasks, so simply start whatever is on our minds to start. The journey of a thousand miles begins with a single step. But if you are overly focused on the journey and all that it will take to get to your goal, you never take that first step.

He can also work to open doors that are closed to us such as doors to a promotion or to a social circle or to a career that seems like it is out of reach to us. Call on Salilus to give you access to those things that are close but seem just out of reach and he can help you to bridge the gap. This can sometimes work in a seemingly miraculous way and help you to seem qualified for positions that you never believed you would be chosen for. In either case, when you work with this power, you may be amazed to find out how far you can go when you are no longer doubting yourself and how quickly you accomplish that thousand mile journey when you stop deliberating and simply take that first step. We are all far more capable than we believe we are.

Sigil of Salilus

JAZER (JAHZ-AIR)

Role: Genius Who Compels Love

Planet: Sun in Virgo

Sephirah: Tipareth

Day: Sunday

Greek God: Helios

Chakra: Heart Chakra (Fourth Chakra)

Powers: Jazer has the power to compel love to blossom between two people by causing them to drop all boundaries and borders between them. To stop worrying about what others might think and releasing judgement of the other person. With the power of Jazer, both people drop their guard around each other and open up. So often we are up tight and on guard in life. The sheer pleasure of being open, unreserved, and completely relaxed around each other causes love to well up deep within their hearts for each other. There is a sense of overflowing warmth that naturally arises when we stop being so uptight, restricted, and judgmental around others. From that warmth, love is naturally born.

This power creates an openness of heart and mind between two people. When two people both open their hearts and minds to each other it creates a sacred spaciousness between them in which their two hearts begin to beat as one. Be careful who you direct this power towards because it is exceptionally strong and long lasting. When effective, the energy of Jazer creates a powerful pull in your hearts towards each other like the pull of the soul towards its heavenly home. It is a pull that causes your hearts to resonate on the same frequency. And in that harmonic frequency, an enduring love is born.

SIGIL OF JAZER

GENII OF THE SEVENTH HOUR LIBRA

TABRIS (TAH-BREEZE)

Role: Genius of Free Will

Planet: Moon in Libra

Sephirah: Yesod

Day: Monday

Greek God: Selene

Chakra: Sacral Chakra (Second Chakra)

Powers: When we are caught up with worrying about how to please others and how to ensure we can please everyone we can never fulfill our true will. It is nearly impossible to live our true will, chase our dreams, and follow our passions without stepping on toes. If a desire to please others and live in harmony is preventing you from doing what you desire to do, call on Tabris. She has the power to make you resolute, determined, and focused on fulfilling your will in all things. This doesn't make you a jerk or uncaring. This makes you like a warrior's arrow, slicing through the air towards its target. You don't set out to hurt anyone but neither are you overly afraid of offending those who stand in your path.

Tabris has the power to erase timidity and the tendency to be worried about "rocking the boat." She gives us the power to stand up for ourselves. To feel free to do what we want to do and be who we want to be. This is an act of love for ourselves. For how can we love or help others if we don't love and help our self first? In this sense, Tabris can also give us self-confidence and self-assurance.

SIGIL OF TABRIS

SUSABO (SUE-SAH-BOH)

Role: Genius of Voyages

Planet: Mars in Libra

Sephirah: Geburah

Day: Tuesday

Greek God: Aries

Chakra: Root Chakra

Powers: If you ever find that you struggle to get things done whether it is due to procrastination, indecision, or fear of failure, Susabo can help. He gives the power, focus, and drive to accomplish all of our goals and aspirations. This is a power that allows you to decisively choose what you desire and then to pursue that goal with confidence and relentless determination. Susabo gives us a sense of direction in life. If you are ever unsure of what step to take next in any endeavor in your life, this genie has the power to bring mental clarity and wisdom so that you can see that best path to take that will lead you towards the fulfillment of your desires. The power to choose can mean the difference between success and failure, wealth and poverty, a loving romance or loneliness. Anytime you are called to make a choice and need a greater sense of direction, call on Susabo to illuminate your path and guide you on your journey to new horizons in your life.

SIGIL OF SUSABO

EIRNILUS (AIR-KNEE-LUHS)

Role: Genius of Fruits

Planet: Mercury in Libra

Sephirah: Hod

Day: Wednesday

Greek God: Hermes

Chakra: Third Eye Chakra (Sixth Chakra)

Powers: Sometimes no matter how well we thought we had prepared for something, our efforts do not bare fruit. In other words, we fail. However, as long as we continue to move forward, treating every failure as a lesson and correcting our course, we will succeed. Be that as it may, proper planning is essential to the successful execution of our plans and the fulfillment of our goals and desires.

Eirnilus is a genie who can help us materialize our dreams and desires by enabling us to see all sides of an issue and make careful, precise plans. Whether you are planning to ask someone on a date, taking a test that will decide your career, or making any other important decision, call on Eirnilus to give you the wisdom on how to proceed the best, to break the ice of indecisiveness and reveal to you what the next step is to take that will bring you the most success. With solid and insightful planning, we may accomplish in a single action what it takes others many actions to complete. With the power of Eirnilus, all of your actions and decisions may bear fruit. Calling upon this genie may save you months of wasted efforts and maximize your effectiveness in all that you do whether in speech or in action.

SIGIL OF EIRNILUS

NITIKA (KNEE-TEA-KAH)

Role: Genius of Precious Stones

Planet: Jupiter in Libra

Sephirah: Chesed

Day: Thursday

Greek God: Zeus

Chakra: Throat Chakra (Fifth Chakra)

Powers: Libra is ruled by Venus which represents harmony, luxury, and beauty. Jupiter represents good fortune, luck, wealth, and expansion. It is said that all good things in life come to us through Jupiter and that all luxury and pleasure comes to us through Venus. Nitika is the genius that represents the expansion of luxury, beauty, pleasure, wealth, and all good and life sustaining things that flow into our life from the universe. This is the true meaning of "genius of precious stones".

Nitika has the power to bring not only money and wealth flowing into our life but also an abundance of beauty, pleasure, and items of luxury as well. When called upon, Nitika is known to act fast and effectively and bringing to us the needed money that we request of him. Although his powers to bring luxury and beauty of all kinds flowing into our life often goes overlooked.

Each of these genies represent the powers of our soul manifested. This is the power of our soul that has the ability to banish poverty and lack and achieve financial and material success in the physical world. Drawing upon the inner wealth which continuously pours forth from the grace and bounty of the Source of the universe, Nitika funnels the prosperous energy and potent help of the Source which pours down from what Kabbalists call the Pillar of Mercy on the Tree of Life (Etz

Chaim).

SIGIL OF NITIKA

HAATAN (HAH-TAHN)

Role: Genius Who Conceals Treasures

Planet: Venus in Libra

Sephirah: Netzach

Day: Friday

Greek God: Aphrodite

Chakra: Solar Plexus Chakra (Third Chakra)

Powers: The spirit behind all treasures is the spirit of beauty. Beauty is a reflection of our divine source. All that is held dear and revered as sacred or as a treasure is born from this spirit of beauty. This includes, art, philosophy, music, love, romance, dance, and all things that bring juiciness to life and make it worth living. This spirit forms a sort of yin and yang relationship with Nitika, the previous genie. Nitika represents material wealth. Haatan represents spiritual wealth. Spiritual wealth is what truly creates the value of all that we treasure and hold dear.

The reason that we desire love, music, art, celebration, and money is not for the objects themselves, but for the spiritual joy, emotional upliftment, and inner pleasure that they bring. Material treasures are just like the outer shell, like a cup. The joy, and pleasure that they bring is like the water that is poured into a cup. Hataan represents this water, which is the spiritual essence that gives all things of beauty and all treasures their true value.

In practical terms, you can call on Hataan in the creation of art, to infuse it with beauty that others will feel. You can infuse your relationships (romantic or otherwise) and interactions with people with this spiritual beauty and thus greatly enhance your interactions with those whom you come into contact with. If you create music, sculpture, dance choreography, jewelry, or any other form of art, this spirit of beauty can infuse your work with that special quality, that fifth element which makes a work of art into a genuine masterpiece that conveys spiritual beauty and uplifts the hearts of the beholders. Of course, this power does not increase your technical skills so you will still have to practice and work on technique. But Hataan can infuse soul into all that you do and create.

SIGIL OF HATAAN

HATIPHAS (HAH-TEA-FAHS)

Role: Genius of Attire

Planet: Saturn in Libra

Sephirah: Binah

Day: Saturday

Greek God: Kronos

Chakra: Crown Chakra (Seventh Chakra)

Powers: In delicate or compromising situations, it can be difficult know how to act, what to say, and what moves to make next. Make a wrong step, and the situation can come collapsing down around you. Make the right step, and the situation can resolve harmoniously for all involved. This may be a power that you do not use very often unless you work in an industry where you deal with such situations frequently. But when you do encounter such a situation, Hatiphas can bring swift help that comes as a great relief. When you find yourself in such a situation, call on Hatiphas with the request for wisdom to resolve the situation harmoniously.

The second power of Hatiphas is the ability to see the truth of a matter or situation as it truly is. This power can be of invaluable help in a large number of situations. It allows you to perceive the true intentions behind decisions that others make, revealing their genuine thoughts or true character. It allows you to see beyond all manner of superficialities and intuitively see the true heart of a person or situation for what it really is so that you may adjust your own behavior and decisions accordingly.

SIGIL OF HATIPHAS

ZAREN (ZAH-RIN)

Role: Avenging Genius

Planet: Sun in Libra

Sephirah: Tipareth

Day: Sunday

Greek God: Helios

Chakra: Heart Chakra (Fourth Chakra)

Powers: Zaren is a genius with the power to restore harmony and balance on all levels in relationships. All fights are essentially based on misunderstandings. Where there is understanding between two people, there can be no fight. When misunderstanding compounds upon misunderstanding it creates wars and solid walls are raised and lines are drawn between people. Zaren has the power to restore harmony and balance to relationships by restoring understanding between two fighting parties. He does this by opening their hearts and minds to each other and creates an opening within the conflict for resolution to come about. This works for all business and personal relationships.

Zaren has the power to heal emotional scars and wounds in a relationship both old and new. Shedding the light of understanding on issues at the heart of a dispute so that it can be brought to the surface in a gentle and loving way and healed. Just like a flower softly blossoming in the warming rays of the sun. Call on Zaren to bring a gentle resolution to all disputes.

SIGIL OF ZAREN

GENII OF THE EIGTH HOUR SCORPIO

ZEIRNA (ZAY-AIR-NAH)

Role: Genius of Infirmities

Planet: Moon in Scorpio

Sephirah: Yesod

Day: Monday

Greek God: Selene

Chakra: Sacral Chakra (Second Chakra)

Powers: If you have ever been sad or depressed about something, you will know how weak your body suddenly feels. You just want to sit down or lay down. Yet when you are angry or excited about something your entire body feels energized and ready to go at a moment's notice. That is the energy that Zeirna has the power to bring. Zeirna is a genie of regeneration. If you have suffered an emotional setback, or are feeling depressed and emotionally or mentally worn down, call on Zeirna. Her energy is like a warm and gentle rush of revitalization flowing through you. Gradually you may feel your energy of heart and mind returning and you feel energized and ready to take on whatever life brings you.

This genie is good for post-breakup blues, and any other kind of sadness or general lower emotional states you might feel. If you need to raise mental energy to complete a project or to focus for extended periods of time, Zeirna can also help with this as she raises your overall energy to a higher level to enable you to handle the demands of whatever situations you encounter with zest and gusto. So if life tackles you and takes you down, rebound immediately by calling on this powerful genie, she will gladly revitalize and reenergize you as well as support whatever efforts that you are making to progress in life.

SIGIL OF ZEIRNA

TABLIBIK (TAH-BLEE-BIK)

Role: Genius of Fascination

Planet: Mars in Scorpio

Sephirah: Geburah

Day: Tuesday

Greek God: Aries

Chakra: Root Chakra

Powers: Tablibik's energy is intense and explosive. This is the power of passion harnessed. His mighty powers work in two ways. If you are working on accomplishing a project and you need extra power and an extra push to continue working on the project until it is done, call on Tablibik to give you that push. He will give you an intensity of energy and focus similar to a genius at work. This won't make you more intelligent or intellectually capable, but it will give you a raw motivation, an animal-like hunger to complete the task you are focusing on and not give up until it is done. This power can be invaluable to procrastinators or those who start things and don't finish them. As well as for tackling boring taks. This is the drive and willpower of great entrepreneurs and great athletes who don't allow failure to stop them and keep getting up no matter how many times they fall down. This is the energy that all great boxers thrive on when in the ring.

The second way this power works is by taking this passionate intensity and turning it outwards to influence others. This won't work with everyone you come into contact with, only with those who would be receptive to your influence. This power works by creating an aura of attraction and fascination around you. This is a primal magnetism that draws others towards you. This is also known as charisma. It is that special force of attraction that goes beyond words or understanding that pulls people to like or even love and desire you just by your sheer presence alone. This power works best when used for general attraction for friendship or to attract a new lover. It doesn't work as well when directed towards a specific person or people who see and interact with you on a daily basis as their preconceived notions of you can block the influence. Therefore, it takes more effort and energy to make this work on people you know, but works readily with people you are meeting for the first time or those you haven't seen in a long time.

SIGIL OF TABLIBIK

TACRITAU (TAH-KRIH-TAO)

Role: Genius of Goetic Magic

Planet: Mercury in Scorpio

Sephirah: Hod

Day: Wednesday

Greek God: Hermes

Chakra: Third Eye Chakra (Sixth Chakra)

Powers: Tacritau is a very powerful genie that holds power over and even thrives in all dark magick, goetic magick, and shadow aspects of the universe. He represents Mercury in Scorpio. Mercury is the planet ruling over magick and all forms of the occult, philosophy, and hermetic sciences. Scorpio is the sign of the Zodiac who is completely comfortable with and loves all dark and taboo things, including the occult and has no fear with confronting any one or anything no matter how dark or seemingly scary it is.

Tacritau combines these two powers for the purpose of giving us the power to directly face and work with the powers of darkness in this universe. If you are working with any forms of dark or goetic magick, calling on this genie can give you the bravery and spiritual power to confidently handle the dark energies manifesting through your work. You can fearlessly speak with demons and bid them to do your will. This power is very valuable if you have a fear of working with darker forms of magick. Tacritau will give you a calm and steady control in your workings and help you to handle the powerful energies of darkness while maintaining the integrity of your mind and emotions and thus keeping you safe. With this power you can master goetic magick and the demons and spirits you call on will respect your calm authority.

Tacritau also empowers you to do shadow work. Shadow work involves facing down the dark aspects of our psyche that hold us back from want to accomplish in life, sabotaging our life due to fears, phobias, and all types of negativity below the surface of our conscious mind, our subconscious. It is typical to ignore these darker aspects of our self by watching tv or indulging in other mindless distractions. We love to avoid facing our self. Tacritau gives you the power to dive deep into the darkness of your subconscious mind, to confront your own internal demons and bring healing to them. It is said that our inner demons only want to be acknowledged and that once we do that, they will transmute into light, inner power, and spiritual strength. This is the work of inner alchemy and Tacritau is a master of this work.

SIGIL OF TACRITAU

SUPHLATUS (SUE-FLAH-TUHS)

Role: Genius of the Dust

Planet: Jupiter in Scorpio

Sephirah: Chesed

Day: Thursday

Greek God: Zeus

Chakra: Throat Chakra (Fifth Chakra)

Powers: Dust represents a particle that obscures and hides a surface. When a surface or an object is covered with dust, it means it is hidden from view and we can not see it for what it truly is. Suphlatus is a genie of deep research and true perception. He gives us the power to clear the dust off of any subject or situation and get to the very heart of a matter. To understand a thing, situation, or person for what they are, without delusion. He gives us the power to go beyond surface appearances and the false façade people put up to keep others out.

If you are researching something, call on this insightful genie to help you to understand your subject matter fully. If you want to understand another person on a deeper level, Suphlatus can give you a penetrating insight into them. This power can also be turned onto yourself as well so that you can know yourself and therefore achieve greater success in all that you do in life.

SIGIL OF SUPHLATUS

SAIR (SAH-YEAR)

Role: Genius of the Stibium of the Sages

Planet: Venus in Scorpio

Sephirah: Netzach

Day: Friday

Greek God: Aphrodite

Chakra: Solar Plexus Chakra (Third Chakra)

Powers: At its heart, magick is not only about obtaining power over life, but about spiritual evolution. Spiritual evolution involves gaining control over the base, animal nature of our being and the negative energy that it can produce. Sair is a genie that gives us the power to have penetrating insight into our lower, animalistic, base nature and its tendencies towards selfishness, violence, and every other ego based vice that hinders us from spiritual growth. Sair helps us to gain control over the negativity of our ego so that we can make spiritual progress. This is the power of spiritual alchemy which the ancient sages practiced and depicted as the changing of lead to gold. Lead represents our base, carnal nature and gold represents our higher self, our spiritual or divine nature. Sair is capable of helping anyone who calls upon her to raise their spiritual vibrations to a higher level of love, peace, and joy.

Sair also rules over sexuality. If you feel afraid or ashamed of your sexuality, or feel sexually blocked then Sair can remove that sexual timidity. She has the power to help us connect to our powerful, primal sexual energy. This energy is like the spiritual fire that has the power to convert the lead of our base, animal nature into the gold of our divine nature. Sair will gladly help you to use your sexual energy to fuel your spiritual evolution. This power lends itself well to tantric sexuality of which Sair is also a master of. There is a wealth of possibility here with this genie.

SIGIL OF SAIR

BARCUS (BAR-KUHS)

Role: Genius of the Quintessence

Planet: Saturn in Scorpio

Sephirah: Binah

Day: Saturday

Greek God: Kronos

Chakra: Crown Chakra (Seventh Chakra)

Powers: Barcus is a genie with the powers of transmutation. Often in life we get weighted down with heavy vibrations, negative thoughts and emotions, doubts, and fears. These negative vibrations have the effect of slowing us down. We may often try to repress these negative feelings and emotions but that only compounds them within us until they manifest later as some form of physical, mental, or emotion imbalance.

Everything is just energy. Whether initially seen as being positive or negative, energy is energy. Barcus allows us to change repressed and negative emotions, thoughts, and energies back into a state of pure energy that we can use for our spiritual growth. This is the power to release all of that darkness that gets trapped and held deep inside of us. This is like a deep, spiritual cleansing process. Be patient with yourself and give yourself time and space when you work with Barcus as old negative or charged emotions, memories, thoughts, and feelings come to the surface to be transmuted into light and energy.

This may not be a power that you use often. Some like to work exclusively with Barcus over the period of a month, calling on him during meditation and then allowing things to rise to the surface, noticing what emotions and thoughts rise to the surface to be dealt with and released. Others prefer to use this power only when they feel negative thoughts, emotions, or beliefs that they wish to release day to day. The choice is yours.

SIGIL OF BARCUS

CAMAYSAR (KAH-MAY-ZAR)

Role: Genius of the Marriage of Contraries

Planet: Sun in Scorpio

Sephirah: Tipareth

Day: Sunday

Greek God: Helios

Chakra: Heart Chakra (Fourth Chakra)

Powers: Camaysar is a genie that brings balance and harmony to extremes. This makes this him incredibly versatile in his powers. If you are struggling and are in the depths of poverty, you can work with Camaysar to help you to find a way out and restore balance to your financial life. If you are lonely, he can help you to attract friendship as well. On the other hand if your life is too busy and crowded, he can help you to find time to relax, slow down, and find peace. Or if that is not possible he will help you find balance within your busy situation.

Camaysar also has the ability to restore balanced communication and contribution within a relationship so it is an even give and take with your partner on all levels. If you are feeling work out and low on energy, call on Camaysar for an increase in energy. You may find your energy naturally increases on its own in the coming days or you may find yourself led to certain foods and dietary changes that have the same result of increasing your energy. Anytime you need balance in any area of life, call on Camaysar to restore harmony. Be open to any changes he may suggest that you make by listening to your intuition and noticing what you are drawn to buying, seeing, saying, or doing.

SIGIL OF CAMAYSAR

GENII OF THE NINTH HOUR SAGITTARIUS

PHALGUS (FALL-GUHS)

Role: Genius of Judgement

Planet: Moon in Sagittarius

Sephirah: Yesod

Day: Monday

Greek God: Selene

Chakra: Sacral Chakra (Second Chakra)

Powers: If you ever feel stuck and unsure of how to proceed in a project, endeavor, or any aspect of life then call on Phalgus. She is a powerful genie that can help us make plans, preparations, and decisions that have the potential for success. If your way forward feels blocked, the powers of Phalgus act the same way as a road opening ritual. She will gladly give you the understanding of how to move forward and get through or around obstacles the easy way. This takes away a lot of the struggle that we would otherwise experience by making the wrong choices or trying to solve the problem on our own.

She is able to give you the clarity and insight of mind and the intuition in your heart to make the right and best judgements regarding any person or thing in your life so that you can meet with success in all that you do.

SIGIL OF PHALGUS

THAGRINUS (TAH-GRIN-US)

Role: Genius of Confusion

Planet: Mars in Sagittarius

Sephirah: Geburah

Day: Tuesday

Greek God: Aries

Chakra: Root Chakra (First Chakra)

Powers: Sometimes in life it can seem as if nothing is going your way. People may be at odds with you, your projects fail, and there is just a general restless unproductiveness. If you find yourself in such a situation, call on Thagrinus. This genie has the power to quite simply, make things go your way. He can help you to win people to your side and help you with winning any sort of competition or debate you are having with another person, getting them to agree with your point of view. He can also give you what may seem like good luck as you pursue projects as everything will begin to become organized and line up for you in the projects you have undertaken. This genie puts you into a flow state in which you become hyper productive and are able to accomplish whatever you put your hand to with a grace that borders on good luck and perfect preparation.

SIGIL OF THAGRINUS

EISTIBUS (AYE-STEE-BUS)

Role: Genius of Divination

Planet: Mercury in Sagittarius

Sephirah: Hod

Day: Wednesday

Greek God: Hermes

Chakra: Third eye (Sixth Chakra)

Powers: Eistibus has the power to open you up to the flow of psychic information. This power can be a great help in performing divination as the name suggests. It works by stimulating and opening your Third Eye which is the eye of spiritual perception. When you work with Eistibus, ask him to give you accurate and insightful psychic perception and then pay close attention to your thoughts, even seemingly random ones during divination sessions and throughout the day. You will find that you may get uncanny insights about people or events that prove to be true. Some people begin to have prophetic dreams when working with this genie although you will have to decipher the imagery to see what it means.

If you work as a tarot reader or do any other psychic work, this genie will prove to be invaluable to you as you may find your rate of accuracy and clarity of insight skyrocketing under his influence.

SIGIL OF EISTIBUS

PHARZUPH (FAR-ZUFF)

Role: Genius of Fornication

Planet: Jupiter in Sagittarius

Sephirah: Chesed

Day: Thursday

Greek God: Zeus

Chakra: Throat Chakra (Fifth Chakra)

Powers: Pharzuph is the genie who inspires broadminded openness and goodwill between people of different religions, philosophies and ways of life. He inspires open minded curiosity and tolerance amongst people of differing viewpoints. He has the power to bring harmony and union. He also inspires open communication which results in the ability to solve issues and disputes of all kinds. This power is good for bringing truth, justice, balance, and harmony to any situation so that all involved will experience a harmonious resolution of their problems.

If you want to find out hidden secrets someone is keeping from you or to find out how they truly feel about you or a subject, call on Pharzuph to cause them to reveal their hidden thoughts.

SIGIL OF PHARZUPH

SISLAU (SEAS-LAO)

Role: Genius of Poisons

Planet: Venus in Sagittarius

Sephirah: Netzach

Day: Friday

Greek God: Aphrodite

Chakra: Solar Plexus Chakra (Third Chakra)

Powers: Sislau is a genie of discernment in relationships. As mentioned earlier in the book, life is all about relationships. Relationships to our boss, house, job, car, parents, and so on. If we enter into a relationship that is harmful for us then our life could be ruined or at the very least greatly inconvenienced. Sislau gives us the power to know what relationship, endeavor, or purchase would be beneficial to us or harmful to us before we pursue it. This comes as an intuitive knowing by regulating our desire. If it is good for us, we may feel our desire for it increase. If it is bad for us Sislau will naturally lessen our feeling of desire for it. An easy way to use this power is to rate your level of desire on a scale of 1 – 10. After you call Sislau, notice if your desire grows higher or gets lower. If it is lower then Sislau is telling you that the relationship is not good for you. If it grows more, then he is indicating it will be beneficial. This power reminds me of a king's guard who eats the king's food first to ensure it is not poisoned before giving it to him. This power can potentially save you years of emotional, financial, or even spiritual trouble.

SIGIL OF SISLAU

SCHIEKRON (SHAY-KRON)

Role: Genius of Bestial Love

Planet: Saturn in Sagittarius

Sephirah: Binah

Day: Saturday

Greek God: Kronos

Chakra: Crown Chakra (Seventh Chakra)

Powers: Ever tried to pull a dog or any other animal in a direction they don't want to go? No matter how hard you pull, they won't budge and they will resist with all their strength. The phrase, "stubborn as a mule" comes to mind. Well, our physical body is just like that. Just like a stubborn animal, it can be downright impossible sometimes to force our self to get up and workout, clean the house, stop a harmful habit, or stop eating unhealthy foods. This is because our body is as stubborn as an untamed animal, a rebellious animal.

If you are struggling to have more discipline and control over your mind (there is a reason Buddhists call it they "monkey-mind"), or your body then call on Schiekron. He is a genie that has the power to bring unity and harmony to the mind, body, and spirit by teaching us to rule over our mind and body with the power of our spirit. When we gain this control, there is nothing that we cannot accomplish. We will be able to break stubborn habits, go into deep meditation, lose weight or gain muscle, develop psychic abilities through limitless concentration, enhance your magickal abilities through greater focus and willpower, and many, many more benefits that come when we finally gain control over our stubborn animal-like lower nature.

SIGIL OF SHEIKRON

ACLAHAYR (AHK-LAH-HAH-YER)

Role: Genius of Sport

Planet: Sun in Sagittarius

Sephirah: Tipareth

Day: Sun

Greek God: Helios

Chakra: Heart Chakra (Fourth Chakra)

Powers: Aclahayr is a genie of great physical energy. He is body, adventurous, confident, and overflowing with energy. When you think of great athletes, they embody the qualities that Aclahayr represents. You can call upon this genie to restore your energy when you feel worn down and tired. If you feel your life is boring and lacking in adventure, call on this power genie to bring more adventure and excitement to your life. If you are participating in any competitive sports or activities, Aclahayr can give you a strong competitive edge over your competition.

This energy is the direct opposite of being withdrawn, introverted, and shy. So if you need energy to be social, accomplish projects, win a competition, give a presentation, or are entering into a situation where bravery is required then call upon this genie to support and help you. You may feel a great outward flowing energy welling up within you that gives you that extra push that you need. This is a very Yang energy. You will become positive, outward oriented, energetic, and ready to conquer all that life lays in your path.

SIGIL OF ACLAHAYR

GENII OF THE TENTH HOUR CAPRICORN

HAHABI (HAH-HAH-BEE)

Role: Genius of Fear

Planet: Moon in Capricorn

Sephirah: Yesod

Day: Monday

Greek God: Selene

Chakra: Sacral Chakra (Second Chakra)

Powers: Hahabi is a genie with the power to bring relief from fear. If we are feeling uncomfortable or insecure in any situation, call on Hahabi to bring a feeling of comfort, calmness, and safety. Any situation that brings uncertainty about the future can cause us to feel fear. Hahabi has the power to harmonize our mind, slow our thoughts, help us to breathe deeply and restore balance and calmness. This allows us to calmly analyze the situation, to see what is true and what is just a fabrication of our minds, to be clear headed so that we can make the right decisions in our life.

This power works for greater fears and phobias such as the fear of death and for lesser fears such as going on a first date, starting a new job, and so on. Of course lesser and greater is relative depending on the person. But whenever you feel fear or uncertainty, call upon Hahabi to bring relief and restore a feeling of security and control.

SIGIL OF HAHABI

PHLOGABITUS (FLOW-GAH-BEE-TUHS)

Role: Genius of Adornments

Planet: Mars in Capricorn

Sephirah: Geburah

Day: Tuesday

Greek God: Aries

Chakra: Root Chakra

Powers: It seems that nothing in this world maintains a state of perfect equilibrium on its own. Things in our life must be maintained in order for them to keep functioning properly or to improve. Whatever is not well kept or carefully maintained will tend to become worse and degrade. The proper word for this is entropy. To prevent entropy, we must maintain and constant, steady, driven effort to improve everything in our life. This can be tiresome, and even the best of us fall short in one or more areas of life. As a result, our health may begin to decline as we gain weight, our finances may run low, our car begins to malfunction, the house gets messy, or our relationships grow cold and distant.

Phlogabitus is a genie who gives us the power to improve everything in our lives. If you feel that any part of your life is suffering from entropy, call on Phlogabitus to help you restore order and harmony to your life. He has the power to give us the strength, focus, and motivation required to ensure that our life does not fall into disrepair or begin to degrade. This power may help us improve each and every part of our life and keep things running in a smooth and orderly fashion. If we are not steadily improving in every area of our life then we are degrading and declining. Call on Plogabitus to reverse the fall, to stop the descent into disorder, and to reverse it.

SIGIL OF PHLOGABITUS

EIRNEUS (AIR-KNEE-US)

Role: Destroying Genius of Idols

Planet: Mercury in Capricorn

Sephirah: Hod

Day: Wednesday

Greek God: Hermes

Chakra: Third Eye (Sixth Chakra)

Powers: Eirneus is a genie that destroys illusions and gets to the very heart of a matter. He gives us the power to see the truth regarding any situation, person, or information. This power allows us to solve whatever problems arise in our life regardless of how confusing or troublesome they seem. If you have encountered any road block or any troublesome situation in your life and are confused regarding how to proceed. Call on Eirneus to help you sort things out. You may find that you become suddenly very efficient. Regardless of the problem we face, we will be able to formulate a methodical and structured plan to overcome it so that we can achieve success. This is the power of great generals of war and great pioneers and explorers. This is the power of great visionaries and revolutionaries who are able to give form and structure to their visions.

Eirneus gives us the power understand and process large amounts of information and organize it in a harmonious and structured way. This power therefore not only helps us with solving all problems in our life but can help us with our studies and with passing tests and examinations of all kinds. This is the power to become highly efficient and effective in all that you do.

SIGIL OF EIRNEUS

MASCARUN (MAHS-KAH-RUN)

Role: Genius of Death

Planet: Jupiter in Capricorn

Sephirah: Chesed

Day: Thursday

Greek God: Zeus

Chakra: Throat Chakra (Fifth Chakra)

Powers: Mascarun has the power of realism. There are few things that are worse than pursuing a dream that will never come to fruition. Magick is powerful and if we are honest, sometimes can seem downright miraculous. But sometimes we may encounter situations that are like a stone pillar and no matter how much magick we throw at them or how much effort we put into trying to change them or make them work, it is all useless and the situation just can't be changed and won't budge. To continue trying to change a situations that is impossible to change or pursue an impossible dream is to set oneself up for failure and defeat. It is far better to find out what we actually can achieve and pursue that instead.

Mascarun gives us the discernment to know what can and cannot be achieved. He helps us to have a solid, realistic outlook in life and not have our head in the clouds. If we call on Mascarun before pursuing something he will give us an idea of whether it is worth pursuing or if it will be a waste of time. Mascarun can also tell us when a relationship, job, or period of our life is at its end or when there is a potential for further growth. There is a time and a season for everything. Those who seem to have great luck are the ones who can sense what actions or pursuits will be fruitful and which ones are a waste of time and energy.

SIGIL OF MASCARUN

ZAROBI (ZAH-ROE-BEE)

Role: Genius of Precipices

Planet: Venus in Capricorn

Sephirah: Netzach

Day: Friday

Greek God: Aphrodite

Chakra: Solar Plexus Chakra (Third Chakra)

Powers: In relationships with others, sometimes it only takes a single false move or wrong decision to destroy a relationship. Trust is slow in coming and takes a long time to build but it can be destroyed in a single moment. Zarobi gives us the wisdom to protect our relationships from these false missteps, harmful slights, or other harmful words and actions that could potentially damage or destroy a relationship. If a relationship has already been destroyed or harmed and it seems beyond repair however, Zarobi has the power to restore the relationship and help to rebuild the trust that was once shared. This works in all relationships from business to romance.

SIGIL OF ZAROBI

BUTATAR (BOO-TAH-TAR)

Role: Genius of Calculations

Planet: Saturn in Capricorn

Sephirah: Binah

Day: Saturday

Greek God: Kronos

Chakra: Crown Chakra (Seventh Chakra)

Powers: Quite often we hear people talk about what they are going to accomplish in the future or the dreams that they want to make a reality. But then no action is taken. Nothing is done to put those plans into concrete form. The dream simply remains a dream.

Butatar has the power to combat this procrastination. He is the genie who has the power to help us take our dreams and visions and bring them down to Earth and give them concrete form and structure. You may be hesitating on fulfilling your dreams due to preconceived notions of how difficult it will be to fulfill them. Or due to fear of failure and perfectionism. Butatar has the power to break through all of your hesitation and help you get right into the planning stage. He will give you the power to calculate exactly what needs to be done to bring your goals and dreams into reality. This doesn't mean that they will quickly manifest. But it does mean that you will be able to take concrete and realistic steps in the right direction so that slowly and steadily you will be able to see your dream come together into a concrete form.

Butatar, as his name suggests, can also help with mathematical calculations, and with those who work with astrology to understand the charts and make accurate predictions. If you are hesitating asking someone out on a date or anything else you would love to do but are held back by fear from doing then Butatar can help you break through your fears and self-limitations. He can also help you to gain foresight into the future through divination.

SIGIL OF BUTATAR

CAHOR (KAH-HOAR)

Role: Genius of Deception

Planet: Sun in Capricorn

Sephirah: Tipareth

Day: Sunday

Greek God: Helios

Chakra: Heart Chakra (Fourth Chakra)

Powers: Cahor is a genie that gives us the power to see through lies and illusion and see the truth in all things. This power can help you to see beyond the lies of other people and behind the masks that they wear to the truth of who they really are. Cahor shines the light of truth into any matter of inquiry to give you the reality of the person or the situation. He gives the power to develop a strong intuition as well so that you can know the truth of anything beyond words and see beyond the obvious.

If you are working towards a goal or a project, Cahor gives you the power to stay on track and not to become distracted. You will be able to move forward in a slow, steady, determined pace towards fulfilling your dreams and desires.

This power also can help you to see the true potential and future of any relationship whether it is a romantic relationship, business relationship, or the future of your career with a certain company. Cahor will inspire you with an intuitive knowledge of how things are working in the present and how things are likely to proceed in the future.

SIGIL OF CAHOR

GENII OF THE ELEVENTH HOUR AQUARIUS

SISERA (SEAS-AIR-UH)

Role: Genius of Desire

Planet: Moon in Aquarius

Sephirah: Yesod

Day: Monday

Greek God: Selene

Chakra: Sacral Chakra (Second Chakra)

Powers: Sisera is a genie that gives the power of genuine and authentic self-expression. To stay true to our self and our deep and honest desires. If you have ever given up on a desire due to people saying it wasn't realistic or practical and that it wasn't appropriate then you know the pain and frustration that can bring. Sisera helps us to fulfill our desires by helping us to stay true to our heart and follow through on our dreams.

Sisera allows us to love our self for who we truly are and to show our true face to the world unabashedly and without shame. This gives us a feeling of great freedom and self-confidence. This doesn't mean we become unruly or break laws, or rebel against societal structure. This power means that we are able to express our true self in a harmonious way and that self-expression brings success within the society.

This power also can attract others to our unique and individual light. If you are looking for a romantic partner who will see your true self and love you for who you really are then call on Sisera to help you shine in such a way that you attract that person into your life. After that be open to those chance meetings and occurrences that may lead you to a romantic encounter with a special person.

SIGIL OF SISERA

TORVATUS (TOR-VAHT-US)

Role: Genius of Discord

Planet: Mars in Aquarius

Sephirah: Geburah

Day: Tuesday

Greek God: Aries

Chakra: Root Chakra (First Chakra)

Powers: We are all unique and this is something to be proud of. The problem comes when people judge, discriminate, and try to force everyone to conform to their set standards of how people should be. If you ever find yourself put into a situation where you need to stand up for yourself, for what you believe is right, call on Torvatus to give you the power to do so. Torvatus gives us the power to be unique, stand out from the crowd, and stand on our own even if we are going against the beliefs of a great number of people. This is the power of a revolutionary, a non-conformist. When you call upon this power you will be strengthened to right any wrongs that you see in your environment, to protest against injustices that others are being silent about, and to be a powerful force for change.

Anytime you are put in a situation where you need to assert yourself, stand up for what you believe is right, or to channel your anger and outrage at injustices such as in a debate or in an actual protest, business negotiations, or even (if it is unavoidable) a physical fight, then call on Torvatus to give you the focus, power, and strength that you need to come out on top, win, and successfully achieve your ambition.

This is the power to win any fight, dispute, battle, protest, or debate. Call upon the fiery energy of Torvatus and, while a win cannot be guaranteed, he will make success much more likely.

SIGIL OF TORVATUS

NITIBUS (KNEE-TEA-BUS)

Role: Genius of the Stars

Planet: Mercury in Aquarius

Sephirah: Hod

Day: Wednesday

Greek God: Hermes

Chakra: Third Eye (Sixth Chakra)

Powers: Nitibus gives the power to understand metaphysical and spiritual topics such as astrology, divination, spirit evocation, and any other esoteric arts. Nitibus helps us to not only understand these arts and develop our skill in them, but to also understand how to make practical use of them in our daily life. Too many metaphysical practitioners are walking dictionaries of theories and knowledge but when it comes time to actually use it, they don't understand how to do it. Call on Nitibus to bring power to your practice of the esoteric arts and help you to bring power to every area of your life through your spiritual pursuits.

This means Nitibus can add power to your spell-work, enhance the energy of your work with crystals, increase the accuracy of your divination, and even make you more receptive to spirit communication. Whenever you need a boost in your spiritual work or are confused on how it can apply to your actual day to day mundane life, call on this powerful genie.

SIGIL OF NITIBUS

HIZARBIN (HEE-ZAR-BEAN)

Role: Genius of the Seas

Planet: Jupiter in Aquarius

Sephirah: Chesed

Day: Jupiter

Greek God: Zeus

Chakra: Throat Chakra (Fifth Chakra)

Powers: Hizarbin is the genie that inspires visionaries and intellectual or spiritual voyagers. Most people are content to follow the crowd and to do the same things that everyone else is already doing whether it works well or not. Hizarbin empowers visionaries who seek to find new and better ways of doing things in life. This is the genie of inventors whose inspiring ideas make life much easier and more enjoyable for the masses. Think of the invention of the toilet, or of the founding of democracy. The inspiring inventions and revolutionary ideas that Hizarbin offers us can make every area of our life or the life of others much easier and more enjoyable.

If you are suffering from creative restrictions or blockages, or are looking for a way out of your tired, mundane, boring and repetitive routine then call on Hizarbin to raise you up, help you to see your life and the world from a birds eye view so that you can see the larger picture and find new ways of solving stubborn, old problems or outdated mindsets. This power is very useful for overcoming longstanding habits and ways of thinking. This is the power that allows you to expand into new and more exciting areas of life and find new, more efficient ways of doing things.

SIGIL OF HIZARBIN

SACHLUPH (SAHK-LUHF)

Role: Genius of Plants

Planet: Venus in Aquarius

Sephirah: Netzach

Day: Friday

Greek God: Aphrodite

Chakra: Solar Plexus Chakra (Third Chakra)

Powers: Few things in life have more variety of shapes, sizes, color, and functions as plants do. There are a seemingly infinite variety of plants, each one unique in its own way, just like with people. No two people are alike and yet there is a place that each and every one of us belongs. A place that we are nourished and loved and accepted for who and what we are. We cannot rest and feel joy until we find that place or that person who accepts us, loves, us, and nourishes us as much as soil and rain nourishes the plants. If you are searching for a person or a place that will love you for who and what you truly are, where you can put down your roots and settle in securely, then call on Sachluph. She has the power to draw us together with that person with whom we fit together like puzzle pieces. Some would call this our soul mate.

The second power of this powerful genie is to help us find what career or place to live would be best for us and would be the most nourishing of our growth and development in life. When you call on Sachluph, ask her to lead you to the place in life that is best for you.

SIGIL OF SACHLUPH

BAGLIS (BAHG-LISS)

Role: Genius of Measure and Balance

Planet: Saturn in Aquarius

Sephirah: Binah

Day: Saturday

Greek God: Kronos

Chakra: Crown Chakra (Seventh Chakra)

Powers: Baglis gives us the power to ensure our plans are sound and reasonable before we put them into action. He gives us the insight to properly judge and weigh all of our options with a cool-headed logic and rationality that ensures we have a realistic view of the situation instead of charging ahead with reckless passion. This power is excellent for anytime mistake or miscalculation is not an option and would lead to great losses. When a judgement or decision is of the utmost importance and you need to be clear and levelheaded in your decision then call on Baglis. He will guide you to make the best decision possible with the rationality and logic of a great architect, scientist, or mathematician.

If any area of our life is suffering due to a lack of balance, Baglis can show us the best way to restore balance. This power can apply to an imbalance in our diet, relationships, financial management, or time management. This genie can make our life work as steadily, and reliably as the gears of a clock.

SIGIL OF BAGLIS

LABEZERIN (LAH-BAY-ZER-EEN)

Role: Genius of Success

Planet: Sun in Aquarius

Sephirah: Tipareth

Day: Sunday

Greek God: Helios

Chakra: Heart Chakra (Fourth Chakra)

Powers: Success in life relies on many different elements. One of the most important though is the ability to think with a sharp, unique, and original mind. To achieve success we need to come up with unconventional and unique ideas. The key to success if forward movement and innovative progress. Labezerin gives us the power to achieve success in whatever we seek to accomplish by stimulating our mind to find out of the box solutions to problems both old and new. If you feel sluggish and limited in your thinking, and just cant seem to find the best path forward, then Labezerin can empower through mind and thoughts and shine a light on the best path forward.

His power reminds me a bit of the popular image of the person that is deep in thought and then a lightbulb lights up above their head when they come up with a brilliant idea. This is a great depiction of Labezerin's power at work. With his power you can overcome any mental and creative blockages that stand in the way of your success and overcome any roadblocks of any sort. There is always a solution to every problem that we encounter regardless of what area of life the problem arises in. If you are ever stuck with a frustrating problem and feel restricted, call on Labezerin to help you break through it and achieve success in all that you do.

SIGIL OF LABEZERIN

GENII OF THE TWELFTH HOUR PISCES

PAPUS (PAHP-US)

Role: physician

Planet: Moon in Pisces

Sephirah: Yesod

Day: Monday

Greek God: Selene

Chakra: Sacral Chakra (Second Chakra)

Powers: Papus is a spirit of infinite help and nurturing. Her energy feels like a warm, healing blanket that is placed over our heart, mind, and wounds that envelops them in light and brings them to a healthy state of balance. If ever feel imbalanced emotionally or mentally then call on Papus to restore balance. This power works more for inner imbalances than for physical ones. It works if you are feeling worn out, tired, discouraged, lonely, or in any type of mental or emotional pain. Papus brings a deep peace and feeling of comfort that restores our strength and brings us back to our true self so that we gain the courage and strength to once again move forward in life and face whatever life throws our way.

SIGIL OF PAPUS

SINBUCK (SEEN-BUCK)

Role: Judge

Planet: Mars in Pisces

Sephirah: Geburah

Day: Tuesday

Greek God: Aries

Chakra: Root Chakra (First Chakra)

Powers: Sinbuck is a genie that brings open hearted acceptance to all. If we feel that we are being judged and discriminated against or if we are discriminatory of others or being judged harshly or unfairly then call upon Sinbuck. This mighty genie has the power to open the hearts and minds of others and diffuse aggression, violence, and unfair judgements. When people judge each other it creates all types of violence, disparity, and unfairness. Sinbuck has the power to bring complete balance and equality so that we see each other as equals are so that others treat us fairly. You may not often find that you need this power but whenever you are in a situation where you wish to be judged in a kinder light and seen as an equal, call on Sinbuck to open the hearts of others towards you and get them to suspend their judgement.

SIGIL OF SINBUCK

KASPHUIA (KAHS-FOO-EE-AH)

Role: Necromancer

Planet: Mercury in Pisces

Sephirah: Hod

Day: Wednesday

Greek God: Hermes

Chakra: Third Eye Chakra (Sixth Chakra)

Powers: Kasphuia is an awesome genie of great psychic power. Regardless of what you need the psychic power to accomplish, whether it is to empower your divinations, communicate with the dead, hear the voices of angels and demons in evocation, astral travel, constructing a powerful servitor, or an infinite number of other psychic powers, call on Kasphuia. He has the power to open your third-eye, the eye of the spirit, so that your psychic abilities and imaginative abilities are vastly enhanced.

SIGIL OF KASPHUIA

ZAHUN (ZAH-HOON)

Role: Genius of Scandal

Planet: Jupiter in Pisces

Sephirah: Chesed

Day: Thursday

Greek God: Zeus

Chakra: Throat Chakra (Fifth Chakra)

Powers: Scandals happen when a person selfishly seeks to benefit themselves alone without caring about the safety and well-being of other people. Zahun has the power to counteract this tendency towards selfishness. He is the genius of cooperation, empathy, and care and concern for others. He has the power to inspire these attributes within your own heart or within the heart of others towards you. If you need someone to treat you with empathy, kindness, and concern and care about your needs even more than their own then call on Zahun. He inspires others with this kind of care and concern for us so that we can get others to fulfill our needs in a way that is balanced and fair.

SIGIL OF ZAHUN

HEIGLOT (HEY-GLOT)

Role: Genius of Snowstorms

Planet: Venus in Pisces

Sephirah: Netzach

Day: Friday

Greek God: Aphrodite

Chakra: Solar Plexus Chakra (Third Chakra)

Powers: There are few things in the world purer than snow. In snowstorms the ground is blanketed in a blanket of pure white. The world becomes like a fascinating wonderland. The ugly, mundane aspects of life like concrete are covered over in a soft, almost dream-like quality of purity. This is the energy of Heiglot. She has the power to add charm, a dream-like quality of idealistic beauty and romance to our life and our relationships. This has the effect of restoring old, tired relationships with the magic that used to exist when we first fell in love. She can also add this energy into your aura so that others are fascinated by you and attracted to your unearthly and mysterious beauty and charm that they see in you. This is like an aura that makes people look twice at you because they sense something different, a kind of charm that draws them in and makes them desire to know you more.

Heiglot can also restore beauty and fascination to your life if you feel that your life has gotten old, stale, and boring. Call on her powers to restore richness and beauty to your life. This may manifest in a wide variety of ways all with the effect of enhancing your enjoyment of life and making you excited to wake up each day to embrace the day and all the things that it holds for you. Almost like the excitement of a child on Christmas morning.

SIGIL OF HEIGLOT

MIZKUN (MEASE-KOON)

Role: Genius of Amulets

Planet: Saturn in Pisces

Sephirah: Binah

Day: Saturday

Greek God: Kronos

Chakra: Crown Chakra (Seventh Chakra)

Powers: Mizkun is a strong protector. His energy is a forcefield or a shield surrounding us and protecting us from any hurt, harm, or dangers whether they be psychic or physical in nature. Mizkun has the power to banish bad luck and curses. If you wish to protect another person you may request this of him and he will do it. This same power can protect dwellings such as apartments and houses, banish hauntings, as well as banishing the fear of the unknown within us.

If you are in need of protection then call upon Mizkun to surround you with his calming and protective energy. He will banish your fear in the face of danger real or imagined and give you a clear head and heart so that you will be able to respond to any dangers rationally and intelligently. He can also protect your items from theft and vandalism or even to protect your emotions from those who wish to harm you emotionally.

Whenever you need peace, safety, and protection in any form or combination you may call upon Mizkun. He can also charge physical items such as jewelry with his energy of protection so that the wearer will be shielded from whatever danger you intend. No protection is 100% but this power works far more effectively than a casual prayer for protection.

SIGIL OF MIZKUN

HAVEN (HEY-VEN)

Role: Genius of Dignity

Planet: Sun in Pisces

Sephirah: Tipareth

Day: Sunday

Greek God: Helios

Chakra: Heart Chakra (Fourth Chakra)

Powers: With the power of Haven we are able to find perfect balance and harmony in all situations and all places. This is perhaps the greatest power of all of the genies combined. And it is fitting of the final genie in the series. For with this genie, the journey of the soul through the signs of the zodiac finds completion. The powers of Haven represent the culmination of every other power. For the ultimate goal of all magick, of all spirituality, of all religious teachings is the power to achieve a state of harmony and balance between heaven and earth. To be able to go through any trial or difficulty and maintain perfect poise and equilibrium. Haven represents at once the center and circumference of the soul. The pillar that maintains the integrity of the soul through all that it encounters in its journey through the Zodiac on its way back to Source.

Whenever you need balance in any aspect of your life whether that is physical, mental, spiritual, or emotional you can call on Haven to restore balance and strength. This also works to heal and rebalance relationship or situations that have gone out of control. He can restore a calm control back to the situation so that your life will flow smoothly.

SIGIL OF HAVEN

THE PERFECTION OF THE SOUL

When you perform the powerful magick within this book, you are working in worlds of light unseen, drawing upon the hidden forces that make up the very structure and foundation of this universe to shape your world according to your will. That is no small accomplishment. As you grow with the magick and practice more often, you will find that the magick will grow more powerful for you with time. You will be able to accomplish things with it that before you only dreamed of being possible.

This magick goes beyond simply making things happen in the physical realm. This magick, as with all other forms of magick and spirituality is truly about the growth of the soul. Whether you realize it or not, with every spell you cast and every ritual that you do, you are experiencing soul growth. As you shape your life and things situations are harmoniously resolved, you attract the romance of your dreams, receive a flow of wealth in abundance, and attain personal power, you are gaining mastery over your world, over the 4 elements that compose this universe. You are becoming like God.

The truth is that each and every one of us is God. Every soul is a mirror of the Universe. A mirror of the Creator and the Creation. It is our divine birthright to attain power and control over our universe by calling upon the creative forces of the universe freely and fulfilling our will. This is why the angels and names of God respond so readily to us. This is why it feels so good to perform this magick. You are attuning yourself with the cosmos and as you do so, you heal and bring harmony to the Earth and all of humanity. By fulfilling your desires, you are climbing Jacob's Ladder back to God, back to Eden. Just like Hercules journeying through the 12 signs of the Zodiac, you are on a journey back to the ultimate perfection and liberation of the soul from the bonds of matter. You are becoming divine.

EXPLORE MORE MAGICK

If you enjoyed this book, you are sure to love my previous books such as the 72 Angels of Power, where you gain the power to control the 72 Angelic Frequencies that make up the soul. By working with these angels you gain the power to rapidly change reality through access to nearly 1000 unique powers.

https://www.amazon.com/dp/B08FGR72PN

If you enjoyed the style of this magick then you will love Goetic Words of Power. In this book you are empowered to call on the 72 Demons of the Goetia for love, wealth, power, and the fulfilment of nearly any desire you can think of. When you work with the spirits in this book, contact is made fast and the powers called upon swiftly and harmoniously shift your world to manifest your desires for you.

https://www.amazon.com/gp/product/B07VF8XY3T/ref=dbs_a_def_rwt_bibl_vppi_i2

TRISTAN WHITESPIRE

Printed in Great Britain
by Amazon